This Asbestos Work
seeking to become a
as required under fe
manual can be used in either the initial four-day or refresher one-day course.

The procedures and practices detailed in this manual incorporate current technology as of the time this manual was written. The student should be reminded that as technology and regulations change, so do the methods for conducting asbestos abatement. Therefore, it is emphasized that the student must obtain the most up-to-date information available. Your instructor for this course will provide you with changes in the regulations at both the state and federal level.

This Asbestos Worker Manual was prepared by professionals in the field of asbestos abatement and was promulgated by Alice Hamilton Occupational Health Center under EPA Grant #CX-81549-01-0, Karen Hoffman, Office of Pesticides and Toxic Substances of the US Environmental Protection Agency, Washington DC and revised by the Department of Health of the State of Maryland.

This manual complies with the regulations of the (OSHA) Occupational Safety and Health Administration --29 CFR 1926.1101 and the US Environmental Protection Agency (EPA)--40 CFR part 763 and 40 CFR 61. Recommended procedures discussed in this manual go beyond the minimum requirements of various regulations.

Published by ehsMaterials

Additional copies may be purchased from ehsMaterials.com

CONTENTS

HOW TO USE THIS MANUAL

This manual is yours to keep. Use a highlighter during the class and put notes on the sides of the pages to help you remember important information. This will help you when you study for the test at the end of the class. After the class is over, you can use this manual for information about your rights and responsibilities as a worker, the rights and responsibilities of your employer and the legal requirements for safe work.

On the first day of class you will learn about:

How asbestos is identified (Chapter 1: Identification).
How the laws about asbestos work (Chapter 2: Laws).
How asbestos can harm your health (Chapter 3: Asbestos Diseases).
How doctors can help you with medical exams (Chapter 3: Asbestos Diseases).
How to protect yourself from asbestos (Chapter 4: Respirators).

On the second day of class you will learn about:

How a building owner can control asbestos (Chapter 5: Control Methods).
How to keep asbestos out of the air (Chapter 6: Setup).
How to set up a job (Chapter 6: Setup).
How to take off asbestos (Chapter 7: Removal).

On the third day of class you will learn about:
How to clean up after a job (Chapter 8: Cleanup).

On the fourth day of class you will learn about:
Safety on the job (Chapter 9: Safety).
How to do small jobs (Chapter 10: Maintenance).

Each day of class will also give you the opportunity to practice using respirators and the safe work methods you learned about in class. You will practice on <u>non-asbestos</u> materials. You will:

Be fitted with a respirator and practice maintaining it
Build a work room and remove non-asbestos insulation
Use a glove bag to remove non-asbestos pipe insulation
Build an enclosure around non-asbestos support beam.
Build and use a mini enclosure to remove ceiling tiles.
Operate and maintain a HEPA vacuum and negative air machine.
Build and use a decontamination area.
Learn methods to remove floor tiles safely.

Many chapters end with a box called "Key Facts." This tells you the most important ideas and words that are covered in the chapter.

There is a glossary at the end of the manual to help you find the information you need. The glossary on page 171 has definitions of the most important terms used in the manual.

When you see these words in the manual: **have to, must, required, shall,** this is something that the law says you **must** do:

When you see these words in the manual, **can, may, might, suggested,** this is something that is a good idea, but the law does **not** say you have to do it:

ABBREVIATIONS USED IN THE MANUAL

ACM	Asbestos-Containing Material
ACBM	Asbestos-Containing Building Material
AHERA	Asbestos Hazard Emergency Response Act
AL	Action Level
CO	Carbon monoxide
EL	Excursion Limit
EPA	Environmental Protection Agency
f/cc	Fibers per Cubic Centimeter
GFCI	Ground Fault Circuit Interrupter
HEPA	High Efficiency Particulate Air
HVAC	Heating, Ventilating and Air Conditioning
IH	Industrial Hygienist
MSDS	Material Safety Data Sheet
MUL	Maximum Use Level
NESHAP	National Emission Standards for Hazardous Air Pollutants
NIOSH	National Institute for Occupational Safety and Health
O&M	Operations and Maintenance
OSHA	Occupational Safety and Health Administration
PAPR	Powered Air-Purifying Respirator
PCM	Phase-Contrast Microscope

PEL	Permissible Exposure Limit
PF	Protection Factor
PLM	Polarized Light Microscope
PSI	Pounds per Square Inch
SCBA	Self-Contained Breathing Apparatus
TEM	Transmission Electron Microscope
VAT	Vinyl-Asbestos Tile

INTRODUCTION

Asbestos can cause disease or kill you unless you protect yourself

Up until the mid seventies, workers weren't told that asbestos is dangerous. They did **not protect themselves when they were working.** Various sources have estimated that upwards of 12,000 workers will die of asbestos-related diseases every year. Most of these workers died ten to forty years after they started working with asbestos. Asbestos can kill you or your family unless you protect yourself from it. **Fortunately, there are ways to protect yourself and to work with asbestos more safely.**

In **this class, you will learn how to protect yourself.** You will learn how to make your work with asbestos as safe as possible.

This means safe for you, safe for your family, and safe for the environment. If you learn the rules for working with asbestos, you will greatly lower your chances of getting sick years from now. You must work carefully and follow the laws. If you do this, you will also help protect your family and neighbors from asbestos diseases and other ailments related to asbestos exposure.

You will learn how to keep asbestos out of the air. You will learn how to keep asbestos out of your lungs after it gets in the air. You will learn how to keep asbestos from spreading outside of the work area. This manual also has important information about how asbestos may affect your health. It tells you about the special medical exams that are required. It tells you where to go for more information.

Asbestos is found in the air at low levels almost everywhere. Everyone breathes some asbestos just from breathing the air. But asbestos workers handle large amounts of asbestos. Your employer has to give you the right equipment. You have to use the equipment in the right ways to protect yourself.

The more you know about asbestos removal, the better you can protect yourself

CHAPTER 1

IDENTIFYING ASBESTOS

In this chapter you will learn:

What asbestos is.
That asbestos can be dangerous.
When asbestos is dangerous.
How asbestos gets in the air.
Where you may find asbestos.
How asbestos is identified.
About the different kinds of asbestos fibers.

WHAT IS ASBESTOS?

Asbestos is a mineral. It is a natural rock mined from the ground. There are several places like Canada, and South Africa where it is mined commercially. Asbestos is not a man-made fiber. (Fiberglass is a man-made fiber.) Asbestos has been used since Greek and Roman times. More recently, it has been used in building and other materials.

When asbestos is crushed, it does not make ordinary dust, like other rocks. Asbestos breaks into tiny, sharp fibers that are too small to see. You cannot see, feel, or taste asbestos fibers that get into your lungs.

WHEN IS ASBESTOS DANGEROUS?

Asbestos is dangerous when you breathe it.

Asbestos can hurt you when it is in the air and you breathe it.

Asbestos is dangerous when you breathe it. Asbestos fibers are so small they can easily get into your lungs. Asbestos can make you very sick many years after you breathe it. Asbestos will not make you cough or sneeze or itch while you breathe it. But if enough asbestos gets into your lungs, it can kill you many years later.

When asbestos gets in the air, you can breathe it. Sometimes plaster has asbestos in it. If the plaster stays on the wall, the asbestos will not hurt you. If you tear down the wall, the asbestos may get in the air. When asbestos is in the air, it is dangerous.

It is easy to get asbestos in the air. If you handle asbestos at all, it can get in the air. If you

Saw / **Abrade**
Sand / **Grind**
Drill / **Strike**
Nail / **Hit**
Cut / **Rip**
Bump / **Break**
or Tear

asbestos, it can get in the air. Once asbestos is in the air, it can get in your lungs and make you sick.

Asbestos fibers are very small. Many are so small that you can't see them. Asbestos fibers are also very light; they go wherever the air goes. If asbestos is in the air in a boiler room, it can travel through the building. It can go through air ducts, under doors, and down halls and stairs. Asbestos is so light it can hang in the air for days. If you step in asbestos dust on the floor, you may cause it to go back into the air.

HOW MUCH ASBESTOS IS IN THE AIR?

There are ways to measure how much asbestos is in the air. Air pumps pull the air through a small filter. The asbestos fibers stick to this filter. The fibers are counted with the use of a microscope. The amount of air that passes through the pump is also measured. The amount of air is measured in cubic centimeters. A cubic centimeter is about the size of a sugar cube. **Asbestos is measured in fibers per cubic centimeter (f/cc) of air.** This is called **air sampling.** You will learn more about air sampling in Chapter. Even though you cannot see asbestos in the air because the fibers are very small, it can be measured. Remember that asbestos is dangerous when it is in the air.

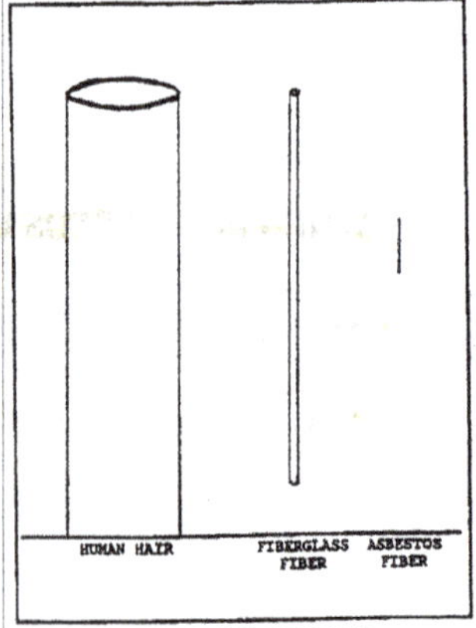

HOW SMALL IS ASBESTOS?

IF ASBESTOS IS SO DANGEROUS, WHY IS THERE SO MUCH OF IT?

Asbestos is a very good fire, heat and sound insulator. It is also very strong. Pound for pound, asbestos is stronger than steel. For example, asbestos is in brake shoes, which need to be strong and resist heat. Asbestos has also been used for many building and construction materials.

Asbestos is most common in:

sprayed-on and troweled on ceiling insulation;
pipe, duct and boiler insulation;
floor and ceiling tiles

Asbestos is in more than 3,000 different products. It is in many building materials. Building materials that are most likely to have asbestos in them are:

fire proofing insulation	**heat insulation**
condensate insulation	**sound insulation**

A lot of asbestos is in old buildings. New buildings built after 1980 don' t have as much asbestos in them. As older buildings do.

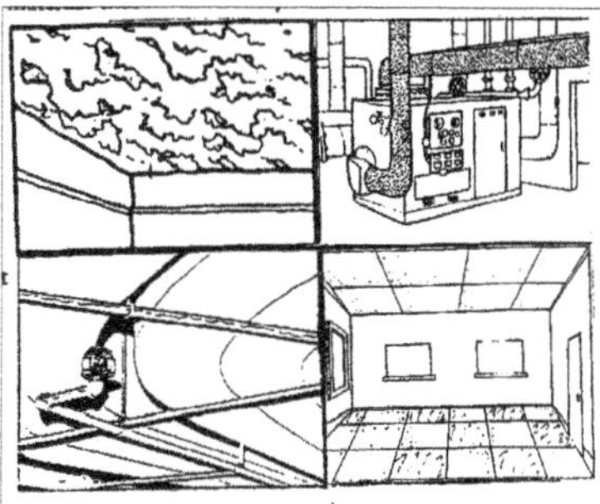

You are likely to find asbestos in:

1. Sprayed-on ceiling insulation
2. Pipe and boiler insulation
3. Duct insulation
4. Floor and ceiling tiles

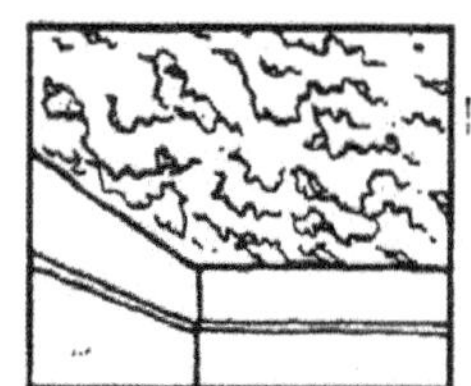

1. Sprayed-on asbestos insulation is usually fluffy material sprayed onto ceilings or beams. Sometimes you can see the insulation from the floor. Sometimes it is covered by ceiling tiles.

2. Asbestos pipe and boiler insulation may be covered with paper, cloth or metal. The insulation may be cardboard-like pipe wrap or cement on pipe elbows. It may also be troweled-on insulation on boilers or boiler wrap.

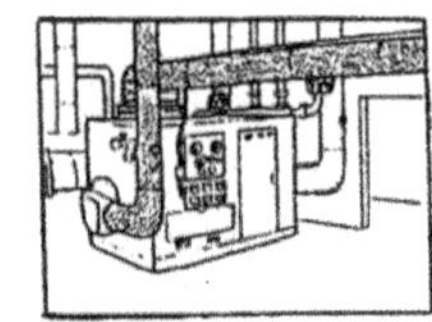

3. Asbestos duct insulation is usually a thin layer of insulation. It is usually painted to match the room. It may be covered with paper, cloth or metal.

4. Asbestos floor and ceiling tile look exactly like non-asbestos tile. Asbestos floor tile is usually either vinyl asbestos tile (VAT) or vinyl composite tile (VCT). Asbestos floor tile can be found in either 9 inch or 12 inch squares. Asbestos ceiling tile is used for sound insulation or for dropped ceilings.

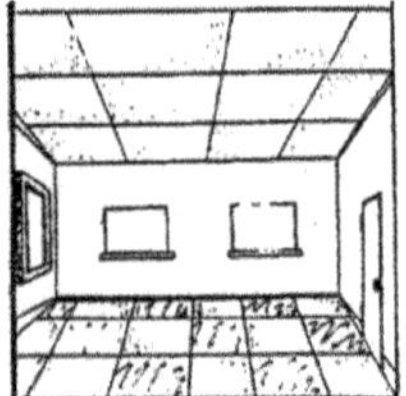

SOME EXAMPLES OF ASBESTOS-CONTAINING MATERIALS (ACM)

- acoustical (sound) plaster
- acoustical (sound) tiles
- boiler insulation
- brake shoes
- ceiling insulation
- chemical tanks
- decorative plaster
- dropped ceiling tiles
- duct insulation
- electrical insulation
- fire blankets
- fire curtains
- fire doors
- fireproofing on beams
- flue pipes
- mastic
- pipe gaskets
- pipe insulation
- roofing felts
- roofing asphalt
- siding
- spackling
- Transite (cement) sheets
- Transite (cement) pipes
- valves
- vinyl-asbestos floor tiles

Asbestos is common in boiler rooms, on ceilings or above ceilings, and wherever pipes are found.

FRIABLE (CRUMBLY) ASBESTOS

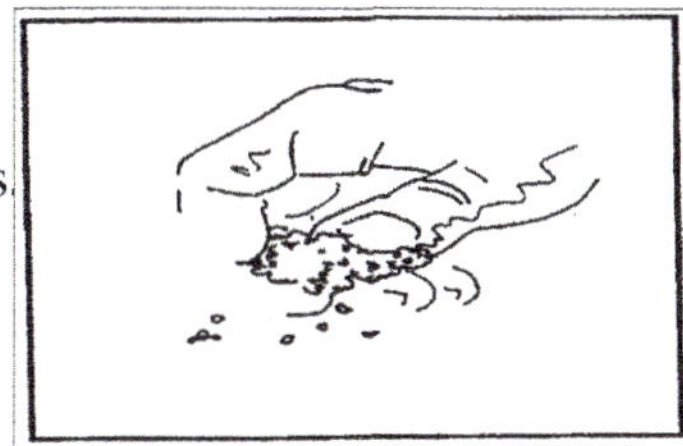

FRIABLE (CRUMBLY) ASBESTOS

Asbestos that can be crumbled to a powder in your hand when **it is dry** is called "friable: (FRY-able) asbestos. (crumbly) piece of asbestos is more dangerous than a non-friable piece of asbestos. The fibers are more likely to release and get into the air.

An example of friable asbestos is sprayed-on ceiling insulation. The insulation may fall off the ceiling and get in the air without even being touched. When someone touches the ceiling asbestos may get in the air. When air blows across it, asbestos may get in the air.

An example of non-friable asbestos is vinyl-asbestos floor tile (VAT) in good condition. If you leave it alone, the asbestos fibers will probably stay in the tiles. But if you saw, drill, or sand the tile, asbestos may get into the air.

IDENTIFYING ASBESTOS

You can't tell if a product contains asbestos just by looking at it.

When you are working in a building, you may not know where all the asbestos is in the building. If you do not know if a material might be asbestos, always assume that it is asbestos. Then check building records or have a sample taken by an accredited asbestos building inspector to find out for sure. You can then check by looking at the lab report(s). Treat all material as asbestos unless it is proven to be non-asbestos by a laboratory test.

IS IT ASBESTOS?

Because you work in a State facility you can look at your facility' s Asbestos Management Plan. The Plan has lab reports kept with it. They tell you whether or not the material is asbestos. Many things look the same as asbestos, whether they have asbestos in them or not. Ceiling tiles made by different companies are made to look the same so they can be replaced. A ceiling tile with 10% asbestos may look exactly the same as a ceiling tile with 30% asbestos. Sometimes asbestos looks white and fluffy. Sometimes it is colored and looks like brown mud. Sometimes it is covered with a paper jacket. The jacket may be painted any color.

Some people say they can tell if something is asbestos just by looking at it. This is not true. No one can tell for sure if something is asbestos by looking, feeling, or smelling. The only way to tell for sure is to send a piece of material to a lab. This is the only way allowed by law.

At the lab, a trained analyst looks at the sample under a microscope. A report will be sent back to tell you if asbestos is present or not. A few building materials have a standard look. Some contain asbestos, some don' t. Corrugated, papery pipe covering, called "air cell", almost always has asbestos in it. Fiberglass, black polyurethane foam, and cork almost never have asbestos in them.

As you can see, asbestos can be in many (but not all) building materials. You need to work carefully around insulation and other building materials that might be asbestos. Remember that not everything has asbestos in it. Glass, gypsum board, fiberglass, polyurethane foam, cork, and ceramic tiles usually do not have asbestos in them. Always treat material as asbestos unless you know for certain that it is not asbestos.

WHAT IS SENT TO A LAB?

To tell whether something is asbestos, an asbestos building inspector trained and accredited under the Model Accreditation Program (COMAR 26.11.23), takes a **piece of the material.** This is called a bulk sample. The inspector repairs the area where the sample was taken. The inspector sends the piece of material to a lab. Samples taken from schools or other public and commercial buildings must go to a National Voluntary Accreditation Program (NVLAP) approved lab. The lab grinds up the **bulk sample** and stains it with dye. The lab then looks at it under a special microscope. It is called a Polarized Light Microscope (PLM).

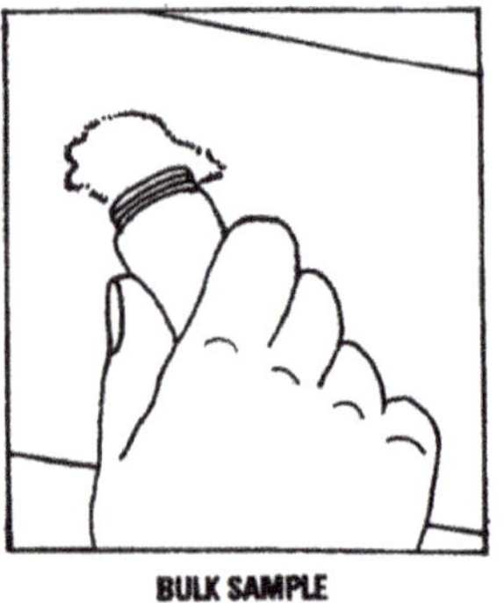

BULK SAMPLE

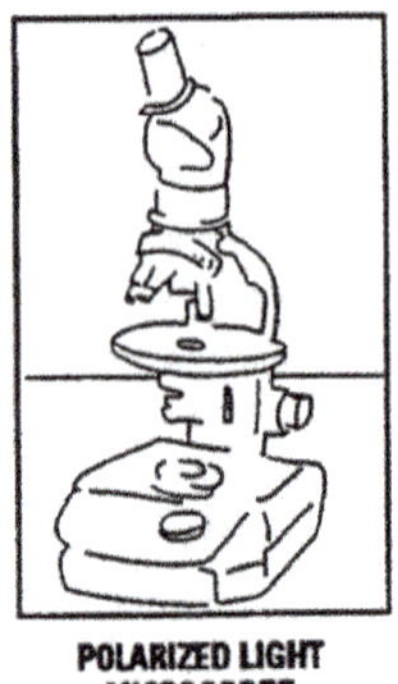

POLARIZED LIGHT MICROSCOPE

ARE THERE DIFFERENT KINDS OF ASBESTOS?

There are six kinds of asbestos fibers. They are all dangerous. The three most common kinds of asbestos fibers are:

CHRYSOTILE (CRY-so-tile)
AMOSITE (AM-o-site)
CROCIDOLITE (crow-SID-o-lite)

CHRYSOTILE asbestos is 80% of all asbestos in buildings. It is known as white asbestos. It is the only member of the serpentine family of asbestos rock. It wets easily.

AMOSITE is less than 15% of all asbestos in buildings. It is known as brown asbestos. It is a member of the amphibole family of asbestos rock. AMOSITE doesn' t soak up water. All asbestos must be wet before you handle it. Wetting asbestos helps to keep the fibers out of the air. A surfactant added to water helps to wet amosite

CROCIDOLITE is less than 5% of all asbestos. It is known as blue asbestos. It is also a member of the amphibole family.

There are three other kinds of asbestos fibers.

Anthophyllite (an THAW-fo-lite)
Tremolite (TREH-mo-lite)
Actinolite (ack-TIN-o-lite)

All asbestos fibers are dangerous.

PROTECTING YOURSELF

Asbestos is dangerous, but you can protect yourself and those around you. Asbestos is dangerous if you breathe it or swallow it. To work safely with asbestos, you have to keep it out of the air. There are lots of good ways to do this. You will learn about them in this class.

You also have to take asbestos out of the air with special filters. Most important, you have to filter the air that you breathe with a respirator--a device that filters the air. You can also wear a respirator that pumps in clean air from outside the work area. You must wear a disposable suit when you work. You must not take asbestos home with you on your clothes. The air that leaves the work area also has to be specially filtered before it leaves the work room. This protects people and the environment outside of the work area.

You cannot tell when asbestos is in the air or is hurting your lungs. **But you can use your knowledge to work more safely and protect yourself. See SEC 4 for more information on protecting yourself.**

IDENTIFYING ASBESTOS

Key Facts

Asbestos is a mineral that breaks down into fibers.
Asbestos is dangerous when it is in the air and you breathe it.
It is very easy to get asbestos in the air.
Wherever air goes, airborne asbestos can go.
Asbestos can kill you, but you can protect yourself.
To work safely with asbestos, you have to keep it out of the air.
When asbestos gets in the air, you have to filter the air with special filters.
You must also protect yourself with respirators and special clothing.
Asbestos is in more than 3,000 different products.

In buildings, you will probably find asbestos in:

- **Sprayed-on ceiling insulation**
- **Pipe and boiler insulation**
- **Duct insulation**
- **Floor and ceiling tiles**

Friable (crumbly) asbestos is more dangerous than non-friable (hard) asbestos. You can' t tell if something contains asbestos just by looking at it. A lab can test a piece of material, called a bulk sample. The lab looks at the bulk sample under a Polarized Light Microscope (PLM). If you do not know whether something is asbestos, assume that it is asbestos until a bulk sample proves it is not.

There are three common kinds of asbestos fibers:

- **CHRYSOTILE (CRY-so-tile) (80% of asbestos in buildings)**
- **AMOSITE (AM-o-site) (hard to wet)**
- **CROCIDOLITE (crow-SID-o-lite)**

Discussion questions

1. Is asbestos dangerous if gets on your clothes
2. Sometimes air ducts are insulated with asbestos. Why is this so bad?
3. Is asbestos floor tile friable? Is this always true?
4. You can' t tell whether a product contains asbestos by just looking at it. Why does this make asbestos more dangerous than other workplace problems?
5. Why is it harder to work safely with AMOSITE asbestos than with other kinds of asbestos? HARD to wet

For more information

*List of asbestos-containing materials, Appendix A to EPA, "Guidance For Controlling Asbestos-Containing Materials in Buildings," (the "Purple Book") EPA Publication No. EPA 560/5-85-024.

*OSHA Asbestos Standard, 29 CFR 1926.1101, Appendix H, "Substance Technical Information for Asbestos."

* "Bulk Sampling," in "Model EPA Curriculum for Training Building Inspectors,"

*The State of Maryland's Asbestos Safety and Health Program's Policies and Procedures Manual.

***Your instructor has copies of this information for you to look at.**

Before 1978 probley HAS it.

TRAINING FACT SHEET

There are a lot of facts that you need to know about asbestos. This fact sheet has been made to help you. It has information you must know. All of the information will be covered in the class. Read this fact sheet over every day. The facts may not make sense when you first start reading them. If you read this every day, it will help you during the class and it will help you pass the test.

I. Federal Government Agencies Involved With Asbestos:

There are three government agencies that deal with asbestos. You will hear about these agencies throughout this training. Here is a list of the agencies and a brief description of each.

1. EPA. The Environmental Protection Agency.

A federal government agency that protects against pollution. The **EPA** makes and enforces regulations to protect the community and the environment from pollution. *(See **SEC 5** for more information about the EPA.)*

AHERA. Asbestos Hazard Emergency Response Act The EPA' s "asbestos in schools" law. *(**See Sec 5** for more information about AHERA.)*

NESHAP. National Emission Standards for Hazardous Air Pollutants The EPA law that covers asbestos as an air pollution problem. *(See **Sec4** for more information about NESHAP.)*

ASHARA. Asbestos School Hazard Abatement & Reauthorization Act.

2. NIOSH National Institute of Occupational Safety & Health

A federal government agency that researches worker safety and health, and reports its findings to OSHA. NIOSH also certifies respirators.

3. OSHA The Occupational Safety and Health Administration

A federal government agency that covers worker safety and health. OSHA makes and enforces regulations (standards) to protect workers. OSHA has regulations about: asbestos, chemical safety, electrical safety, ladders, respirators, scaffolds and many other workplace hazards. *(See **SEC 5** for more information about OSHA.)*

II. Measurement of Asbestos

Airborne asbestos is measured in fibers per cubic centimeter (f/cc) of air. A cubic centimeter is about the size of a sugar cube. The air is checked for asbestos fibers through air sampling methods. *(See the Air Sampling handout for more information about air sampling.)*

OSHA sets limits on the amount of asbestos fibers you can be exposed to during your work. There are two (2) limits that you will need to know. They are the Permissible Exposure Limit **(PEL)**, and the Excursion Limit **(EL)**.

Permissible Exposure Limit (PEL) - 0.1 f/cc

The Permissible Exposure Limit is 0.1 f/cc. It is the average number of fibers in the air over an 8-hour period of time that equals 0.1 fibers/cc.

The PEL is the highest number of fibers in the air (allowed by Law) or a worker to be exposed to. The Permissible Exposure Limit is like a red light. It means stop work.

Excursion Limit (EL) - 1 f/cc

The Excursion Limit is 1 f/cc. It is the average number of fibers in the air over a 30-minute period of time that equals 1.0f/cc.

The Excursion Limit is the highest number of fibers a worker can be exposed to in any thirty minute time period. It is like a red light. It means stop work. The Excursion Limit protects you from large amounts of asbestos exposure in a short time period.

Neither the Permissible Exposure Limit nor the Excursion Limit represents a safe exposure. Any exposure has some risk. Thus, exposure to airborne asbestos fibers must be kept as low as possible.

IV. Respirators

Respirators are used to protect your from breathing asbestos fibers. There are three terms that you need to know to use the information about respirators. It is important to learn these terms so that you know whether you have the right respirator for your asbestos work. These terms are:

1. **Maximum Use Level (MUL)** - the largest amount of airborne asbestos (in fibers/cc) a respirator can handle

2. **Protection Factor (PF)** - the degree of protection of a respirator

3. **Permissible Exposure Limit (PEL)** = 0.1 fibers/cubic centimeter of air

These three terms combine to give you a formula that you can use.

Formula: Maximum Use Level = Protection Factor x Permissible Exposure Limit

MUL = PF x PEL (0.1 f/cc)

How to Use The Formula:

An Example: A powered air-purifying respirator (PAPR) has a protection factor of 100 with the motor on. For every 100 fibers outside, 1 fiber leaks in. When can you use this respirator?

MUL = (100) x 0.1 f/cc **so**

The Maximum Use Level for a PAPR is 10 fiber/cc, **so**

1. Below 10 fibers/cc in the air, a powered, air-purifying respirator is legal. **(However at 10f/cc asbestos fibers become visible and that is not a good situation)**
2. Above 10 fibers/cc the respirator is not allowed. You need at least a <u>Type C Pressure Demand Airline Respirator.</u>

(The State Employees Asbestos Program <u>requires</u> at least a Powered Air Purifying Respirator for Level II building maintenance workers)

CHAPTER 2

LAWS

In this chapter you will learn about:

Regulations and how they are enforced.
The differences between State and Federal asbestos laws.
The government offices that cover asbestos removal.
The laws that protect you on the job.
The laws that protect the environment on the job.

LAWS

The law is one tool for a safer and healthier job. However, the protection furnished by occupational and environmental safety laws depends extensively on how well people comply with these provisions. When it comes to asbestos and other hazardous materials, substantial compliance is not enough. Everyone must do his or her part. For example, if just one individual fails to comply with the requirements, he/she could create conditions that endanger the entire work crew or could contaminate the environment. Thus, it is extremely important for everyone working with asbestos to know the safety and health requirements. Each person must follow them to the letter and should insist that fellow workers also follow the requirements.

Asbestos project supervisors have an ethical and legal responsibility to ensure that work proceeds in a safe manner. The minimum standards for safe asbestos work are prescribed in regulations set forth by OSHA (the Occupational Safety and Health Administration) and EPA (the Environmental Protection Agency). These regulations were promulgated on statutes enacted by Congress, and carry enforcement penalties for non-compliance. There are also State of Maryland Regulations based on laws enacted by the Maryland General Assembly, which both complement and supplement Federal Regulations.

As stated before, these regulations set the minimum requirements to protect workers and the environment from asbestos hazards. They also serve as a competency standard for supervisors. For example, OSHA's asbestos regulations specifically require supervisors to be a Competent Person. By definition, a Competent Person is a knowledgeable person able to identify asbestos and associated safety hazards, prescribe control measures to protect workers and the environment. In addition, to be a competent person, the individual must also have the authority to take prompt corrective actions to eliminate hazards that may arise during the project. It is important to note that the supervisor, as a competent person, may be judged by how well he/she protected workers and the environment, not necessarily on the question did he/she just follow the regulations.

These competency issues are likely to be decided by a jury during a tort liability trial sometime in the future, with the consequences much more severe than any penalty levied by regulatory enforcement officials.

It is also important for supervisors to realize that there are several serious safety hazards at the worksite besides asbestos. These could include heat stress, electrical hazards, fall hazards, confined spaces, lifting and material handling hazards, among others. You need to be competent in addressing these other safety concerns. Before any work commences on an asbestos project, you should assess all the potential safety hazards on the job site, and be sure that appropriate control measures are implemented according to established safety practices in the industry. It is recommended that a copy of the OSHA regulation 29 CFR1926 be checked as part of the project planning process.

Construction Standards

29 CFR 1926.1101

ASBESTOS

Replaced 1926.58 on August 10, 1994; MOSH adoption Jan. 30, 1995.

Applies to:

[(a)]

(1) removal or encapsulation of materials containing asbestos;
(2) construction, alteration, repair, maintenance, or renovation of structures, substrates, or portions thereof, that contain asbestos;
(3) asbestos spill/emergency cleanup;
(4) transportation, disposal, storage, containment of, and housekeeping activities involving asbestos or products containing asbestos on the site or location at which construction activities are performed.

New Definitions: [(b)]

* **Building/facility owner: legal entity, including lessee, which exercises control over management and record keeping functions related to the building or facility.**

* **Disturbance: a Class III operation where contact with ACM or PACM (either accidental or intentional) is or could be released but amount is no more than what will fill a standard size glove bag or waste bag (60 united inches).**
 {NOTE: If amount above is exceeded, the operation becomes a Class I or II job, depending on the type of asbestos disturbed (TSI/Surfacing or Misc.)}.

* **PACM: Presumed Asbestos Containing Material.**

* **Competent person training:**

 If Class I or II work: Supervisor training (5 day);
 If Class III or IV must have O & M course training (2 day).

Permissible Exposure Limits (PELs) of: [(c)]

* **0.1 f/cc, for an 8-hour Time-Weighted Average (TWA); and**
 1.0 f/cc over a 30-minute sampling period called Excursion Limit (EL).
 No more action limit (AL).

Regulated Area: [(e)]

- * an area established and demarcated by the employer where Class I, II, III work is being conducted and any adjourning areas where debris and waste accumulate,
- * where airborne concentrations are or may exceed the PELs,
- * only authorized persons allowed,
- * must wear an appropriate respirator,
- * have appropriate sign and demarcation tape,
- * no eating, drinking, smoking, chewing tobacco or gum, or applying of cosmetics.

NOTE: standard does not address Class IV operations as regulated areas but would be if above PELs.

Competent Person: [(o)]

- * Employer must designate such a person and must have the qualifications and authority to ensure worker safety and health under 1926.20 (b)(2) through 1926.32, which includes:
  - accident prevention program, which includes frequent and regular on-site inspections;
  - education and training program in the recognition and avoidance of unsafe conditions and the regulations applicable to the work environment; safe handling, personal hygiene, and personal protective practices;
  - confined space entry procedures;
  - housekeeping;
  - illumination;
  - fire protection and prevention;
  - first aid procedures; and

- * from the ASBESTOS standard:
  - inspect Class I site at least once per shift or at employee's request,
  - inspect Class II, III, and IV at sufficient enough intervals to assess whether conditions have changed and at an employee's request,
  - set up regulated area, enclosure, or other containment,
  - supervise employee exposure monitoring and ensure it is conducted correctly,
  - ensure employees in containment or using glove bags are wearing respirators and protective clothing,
  - ensure through on-site inspections that engineering controls are working properly and employees are using proper work practices,
  - ensure that employees are using the hygiene facilities and decontamination procedures, and ensure notification requirements are met.

Need for Initial Exposure Assessment (IEA) (personal sampling): [(f)(2)]
Must be conducted by a "competent person" immediately before or at the initiation of the operation. [(b)]

***Exception- Class I jobs must assume > TWA or EL until exposure monitoring conducted and shows < TWA/EL.**

Negative Exposure Assessment (NEA) [(f)(2)(iii)]

For any one specific job, the employer may demonstrate exposures below PELs from data, which is...

- **A.** **Objective data demonstrating that product/material or activity cannot release fibers exceeding PELs; or**
- **B.** **Previous monitoring (below PELs) within last 12 months and the data obtained closely resembles the process, type of material, control methods, work practices, environmental conditions, and training and experience of employees. From this data, there must be a high degree of certainty that exposures will be under the TWA and EL; or**
- **C.** **Results of initial breathing zone monitoring of current job are under the PELs and are representative of entire job.**

CLASSES OF WORK:

Class I: activities involving removal of Thermal System Insulation and surfacing ACM or PACM (Presumed Asbestos Containing Material); [(g)(4)]

***** respirator must be provided and required to be used ***** [(h)]

...if no negative exposure assessment must provide a full face, supplied-air respirator operated in the pressure demand mode and equipped with an auxiliary, positive-pressure, self-contained breathing apparatus;
*****but if exposures are under 1.0 f/cc for an 8-hour TWA, a tight-fitting, full-face piece, powered-air purifying respirator (PAPR) may be used.**

DECON unit: > 10 ft^2 or 25 linear feet of TSI or surfacing is being removed, a 3-stage unit (connected equipment, shower, & clean rooms) is required; When < 10/25, or where exposures > PEL or no negative exposure assessment shall establish an equipment room or area adjacent to regulated area.
Protective coveralls and gloves if over TWA/EL or over 10 SF or 25 LF.

NOTE: If the removal is a glove bag operation, there must be two employees present to perform this activity.

Class II: activities involving removal of ACM other than TSI or surfacing material if not done in an intact state. [(g)(7)]

Examples- removal of wallboard, floor tile and sheeting, roofing, siding shingles, mastics, cutting into fire doors or privy doors.
-respirator must be provided and required usage if asbestos is not removed in a substantially intact state, or not using wet methods, or no negative exposure assessment. [(h)(1)]

Vinyl and asphalt flooring - no sanding, must use HEPA vac, resilient sheeting cutting with wetting at the snip point and wetting during delamination. Rip-ups prohibited. Scraping of adhesive residue and/or backing using wet methods.

Removal of intact tiles only unless can show not possible. If can be removed intact by heating, wet method can be omitted. [(g)(8)(i)]

Care of asbestos-containing flooring material: (1910 - General Industry)

Stripping conducted using low abrasive pad, < 300-rpm buffer, and wet methods.

Burnishing or dry buffing performed only when enough finish so pad does not contact flooring material.

Siding shingles or panels - no breaking, cutting, or abrading unless can demonstrate other methods can not be used. Wetting with amended water. Immediately wrapped or bagged. Disposed at end of each workday. [(g)(8)(iii)]

Gaskets - Removed within glovebag if visibly deteriorated or unlikely to be removed intact. Thoroughly wetted with amended water including residue. Immediately placed in disposal container. [(g)(8)(iv)]

Class III: repair and maintenance operations where ACM including TSI or surfacing is likely to be disturbed (either accidentally or intentionally) and contact can releases fibers. [(g)(9)]

-disturbance is an amount that does not exceed amount contained in one standard-sized glove bag or waste bag (1/3 to 1/2 full) and in no event shall exceed 60 inches in length and width.

-required to use wet methods and to extent feasible, local exhaust ventilation.

-if no sampling data or over PEL' s or no negative exposure assessment, must use impermeable dropcloths and plastic barriers or equivalent and isolate by using mini-enclosures or glovebags.

Class IV: Housekeeping (not cleanup) that takes place in an area after a Class I, II, or III job has been completed. Does not include picking up and bagging of asbestos debris/dust during Class I, II, or III operations.

[(g)(10)]

"Competent person" must evaluate work before being done to assure the work is not another class of work.

-mandated to use wet methods, HEPA vacuums, and promptly clean up debris containing ACM or PACM.

-if TSI or surfacing is accessible during housekeeping operations, other waste and debris is to be considered asbestos containing (contaminated).

Requirements when exposures over the PEL or EL or without a Negative Exposure Assessment:

-regulated area with appropriate sign and demarcation.
-respiratory protection with specific Class and emergency use requirements.
-protective clothing with immediate repairs to rips and tears and competent person to examine once per work shift.
-training, medical surveillance, record keeping.
-competent person: designated by employer with qualifications and authority to ensure worker safety and health and perform inspections of the site.

NOTE: If specific control measures not given, then must use...

A. Use of HEPA vacuums,
B. Wet methods unless infeasible due to hazards of electricity or slips or equipment malfunction,
C. Prompt clean up and disposal of debris in leak-tight containers,
D. Local exhaust systems with HEPA filtration,
E. Enclosure or isolation.

Labels:

affixed to all products containing asbestos and to containers containing asbestos. If feasible, installed asbestos products shall contain a visible label unless has been modified by a bonding agent, coating, binder, or other material and manufacturer can demonstrate that through use, handling, storage, processing, or disposal no release at PEL or EL will occur or < 1%. [(k)(7)]

Previously installed PACM/ACM shall be clearly labeled or signs to notify employees of what materials containing PACM/ACM there are in their building and to entrances of mechanical rooms containing ACM/PACM.

Signs may be used in lieu of labels if contain required label information.

Training: Variable amounts according to Class of work. (k)(9)]

Class I & II training equivalent to EPA' s 4day asbestos abatement worker or
5-day for asbestos supervisor and both include 16 hours of "hands-on".
Class III training equivalent to 16-hour Operations and Maintenance course for EPA.
Class IV training equivalent to 2-hour awareness training course for EPA.

NOTE: Every employee who works with a category of ACM material (roofing, flooring, siding, or Transite) containing asbestos shall receive additional training.

Housekeeping: [(l)]

If using a vacuum, must be HEPA filtered. NO compressed air blow downs of area or tools.

Medical Surveillance: [(m)]

Program for employees for 30 or more days per year engaged in Class I, II, III work (Does NOT apply to Level II workers) or exposed at or above TWA or EL and wear negative-pressure respirators.

NOTE: This does not apply in Maryland where there is no 30 day stipulation.

Initial examination conducted prior to assignment and at least annually thereafter.

Building and Facility Owners must before work subject to this standard is begun: [(k)]

* identify presence, location, and quantity of ACM or PACM at site.
* notify in writing or personal communication:

(A) prospective employers,

(B) employees of employers,

(C) tenants who occupy areas containing such materials.

*** post signs on mechanical room doors that identify type, location, and appropriate work practices to ensure will not disturb ACM/PACM.**

*** affix labels or signs to notify employees of what materials contain ACM/PACM.**

29 CFR 1910.134

RESPIRATORY PROTECTION

Employer' s primary obligation is to control atmospheric contamination by feasible and accepted engineering control methods (for example, enclosure or confinement of the operation, general and local ventilation, or substitution of less toxic contaminants).

When not feasible or while engineering controls are being implemented, appropriate respirators shall be used under the following requirements:

1) **when necessary to protect the health of the employee,**
2) **applicable and suitable for the purpose intended, and**
3) **responsible for the establishment and maintenance of a respiratory protection program.**

Requirements for a minimal acceptable program:

1) **written SOPs governing the selection and use...,**
2) **selected on the basis of the hazards to which worker is exposed,**
3) **instructed and trained in the proper use and limitations, including having it fitted properly, test its face-to-facepiece seal, and wear in a test atmosphere,**
4) **where practicable, should be assigned to individuals for exclusive use,**
5) **regularly cleaned and disinfected after each use,**
6) **stored in a convenient, clean, and sanitary location,**
7) **routinely inspected during cleaning, worn and deteriorated parts shall be replaced, according to the manufacturer's instructions**
8) **appropriate surveillance of work area conditions and degree of employee exposure or stress shall be implemented and maintained on an on-going basis,**
9) **regular inspections and evaluation to determine the continued effectiveness of the program shall be conducted,**
10) **must be medically evaluated to determine if physically able to work and wear respirator(s), considering the conditions in the environment in which the respirator will be worn,**
11) **only approved respirators shall be used and provide adequate protection from the hazard for which it was designed.**
12) **respirators must provide adequate protection from the hazard(s) for which they were designed.**
13) **the employer shall designate a program administrator who is qualified by appropriate training or experience that is commensurate with the complexity of the respiratory program to oversee the program and conduct the required evaluations of program effectiveness.**

29 CFR 1910.1020

ACCESS TO EMPLOYEE EXPOSURE AND MEDICAL RECORDS

- Provides employees and their designated representatives a right to relevant exposure and medical records.
- Applies to general industry, maritime, and construction employers who make, maintain, contract for, or have access to employee exposure or medical records, or analyses thereof, pertaining to employees exposed to toxic substances or harmful physical agents.
- "Access," means the right and opportunity to examine and copy.
- "Designated representative" means any individual or organization to which an employee gives written authorization to exercise a right of access.
- Employer has 15 days to respond to a request.
- No charge for the first copy and only reasonable administrative cost for copies of the same record thereafter.
- Upon an employee' s first entering into employment, and at least annually thereafter, each employer shall inform employees exposed to toxic substances or harmful physical agents of the following:

  (i) the existence, location, and availability of any records covered by this section;
  (ii) The person responsible for maintaining and providing access to records; and
  (iii) Each employee' s rights of access to these records.

29 CFR 1910.1200

HAZARD COMMUNICATION

- Requires employers to develop, implement, and maintain a written Hazard Communication Program, which describes how the employer will inform employees of this law, its elements, and their rights.
- Includes a list of chemicals that Maryland mandates being called CIL as noted above.

Elements:

Labels and other forms of warning:

Every container, tank, or vessel must have a label identifying the hazardous ingredients and appropriate hazard warnings and manufacturer' s name, address& phone.

NOTE: THERE ARE EXCEPTIONS NOT COVERED HERE

Material Safety Data Sheets:

Must have an appropriate MSDS for every hazardous or toxic chemical on the site and available for employee access.

Employee information and training:

Must be informed of this law and its requirements, what operations where hazardous chemicals are present, and location of CIL, MSDSs, and written hazard communication program.

Must be trained on:

*** methods and observations that may be used to detect the presence or release of hazardous chemicals (monitoring methods, visual and odor detection),**
*** physical and health hazards,**
*** procedures and practices to protect themselves from exposures.**

Environmental Protection Agency (EPA)

NATIONAL EMISSIONS STANDARD FOR HAZARDOUS AIR POLLUTANTS

NESHAP

(CAA) (40 CFR 61 Part M) (1990)
(Revised from 1984)

-Banned asbestos spray-applied insulation, pre-molded insulation (if friable), spray-applied decorative material.
-No visible emissions to the outside.
-Required notification 10 days prior to any removals, demolition, and renovations when asbestos amounts larger than 160 square feet or 260 linear feet or 35 cubic feet.
-Removal and stripping of asbestos made adequately wet and no dropping, throwing, sliding, or otherwise disturbing.
-Use of local exhaust and collection systems (negative air machines).
-Only approved variances for nonwetted renovations and removals when there are safety and equipment damage concerns.
-Defined Category I and II nonfriable RACM (regulated asbestos-containing material) in relation to demolition and renovation operations.

Category I nonfriable ACM includes asbestos-containing packings, gaskets, resilient floor covering and asphalt roofing products.

Category II nonfriable ACM includes any asbestos-containing material, not included in Category I nonfriable ACM, that when dry, cannot be crumbled, pulverized or reduced to powder by hand pressure but mechanical forces during the course of demolition or renovation make them friable. Examples are cement siding shingles and Transite products.

-Established standards for waste disposal for manufacturing, fabricating, demolition, renovation, and spraying operations.
-Training requirements for onsite representatives.

ASBESTOS HAZARD EMERGENCY RESPONSE ACT

AHERA

(40 CFR Part 763, TSCA-- published October 30, 1987; effective December 14, 1987; implementation of MP- May 1989)

-Applicable to private and public non-profit schools through 12th grade (including non-profit nurseries and pre-schools) required inspecting buildings for asbestos presence and condition.
-Local Education Agency (LEA)- Designates a person to ensure implementation of the management plan for the school.
-Must develop and implement updated asbestos management plans.
-Operations/Maintenance Plan and implementation.
-Abatement project planning/supervision. Abatement work done by certified persons who have attended 3-5 day training courses with EPA approval.
-Annual notification to parents and occupants.
-Specific training requirements for accredited persons.
-Required periodic surveillance (every 6 months) and re-inspection (every 3 years) to monitor ACM left in schools.
-EPA was to recommend to Congress to extend this regulation to public buildings.

ASBESTOS MANUFACTURING, PROCESSING, IMPORTATION AND DISTRIBUTION PROHIBITIONS

(TSCA) November 5, 1993
40 CFR Part 763

EPA issued a final rule under section 6 of the Toxic Substances Control Act (TSCA) prohibiting, at staged intervals, the future manufacture, importation, processing, and distribution in commerce of almost all asbestos-containing products, and required labeling of such products in the interim.

On October 18, 1991, the United States Court of Appeals vacated and remanded most of the rule but left intact the portion that regulates products that were not being manufactured, produced, or imported when the rule was published on July 12, 1989.

The six asbestos-containing product categories that are still subject to the prohibition are corrugated paper, rollboard, commercial paper, specialty paper, flooring felt, and new uses of asbestos.

The asbestos-containing product categories that are no longer subject to the rule are: asbestos-cement corrugated sheet, asbestos-cement flat sheet, asbestos clothing, pipeline wrap, roofing felt, vinyl-asbestos floor tile, asbestos-cement shingle, millboard, asbestos-cement pipe, automatic transmission components, clutch facings, friction materials, disc brake pads, drum brake linings, brake blocks, gaskets, non-roofing coatings, and roof coatings. (Thus, it is possible that these products could contain asbestos, even today. Work involving these materials should proceed with caution. The supervisor should either have samples taken by an accredited building inspector or obtain reliable information on the content of these materials before performing work activities.)

ASBESTOS SCHOOL HAZARD ABATEMENT REAUTHORIZATION ACT

ASHARA

Passed by Congress as an interim final rule and amended AHERA' s Model Accreditation Plan
(Effective 10-3-94)

- Clarifies the types of persons who must be accredited to work with asbestos in schools and expanded coverage to public and commercial buildings, i.e., individuals working in public and commercial buildings, must have AHERA accredited training as either a worker, supervisor, project designer, or building inspector, as applicable.

- **Increased the minimum number of hours of training, including additional hours of hands-on health & safety training for abatement workers and contractor/supervisors.**
- **Congress expanded accreditation for inspectors, project designers, workers, contractors/supervisors working in schools, public and private building but did not enact accreditation requirements to management planners working in public and commercial buildings.**
- **Exempted residential properties and dwellings with <10 units.**
- **Defined "small-scale, short-duration activities," where less than 3 square or linear feet did not have to use accredited workers and over 3 square or linear feet would have to use accredited workers.**
- **Certificates for accreditation required issuing provider' s name, address, and telephone number.**
- **Civil penalty of $5000 per day per violation provisions.**

---

1 Level I employees are those workers employed in positions with the potential for asbestos exposure because of work-related activities or location, but who are not required to break, cut into, tear out or otherwise disturb asbestos or asbestos-containing materials.

Level II employees are those workers employed in positions whose job activities may cause them to break, cut into, tear out, or otherwise disturb asbestos-containing materials, or who must work in areas where this activity takes place.

Asbestos Management Plan (AMP): develop and update annually and consist of a safety, health, and equipment program, a training and medical monitoring program, and a statewide operations and maintenance program.

Asbestos Abatement Plan: develop a prioritized schedule of abatement activities.

Safety and Health Program: State employees required to work with asbestos only when incidental to their work and less than 160 square feet or 260 linear feet or 35 cubic feet of ACM per building per year. Exceeding shall be contracted out. Each department/agency shall implement and shall appoint a S&H Coordinator who appoints a S&H Committee. Each facility shall have a S&H Specialist be responsible for their program.

Level II State employees can volunteer to remove ACM if requirements of training, medical monitoring, and PPE usage is in order but only if it is under the 160/260/35 limits for the building. Incentive pay for working with asbestos.

Equipment: provide employees with appropriate respiratory protection [(1/2 face for automotive workers) (PAPR, or Type C, pressure-demand, supplied-air for other designations)] and protective clothing while performing Level II-type activities.

Medical Monitoring and Training: Employees agreeing to work in positions that involve incidental exposure to asbestos shall participate in this monitoring program after successfully completing a formal asbestos training program.

Operations and Maintenance Program: (within the AMP) contains a procedure to locate and identify asbestos in State buildings, and to assess its condition and type; a statewide project schedule for abatement projects; a procedure for performing recurrent surveys and inspections to update existing conditions, and guidelines for preparation and prioritization of contract removals with outside contractors.

COMAR 26.11.21

CONTROL OF ASBESTOS
Updated in (1998)

-Applies to all business entities and local governments.
-State agencies/facilities are exempt from its requirements as per Executive Order however; asbestos work practices performed by State Facilities must be equal to or better than the State regulations.
-Defines "Operations and Maintenance" as removal, encapsulation or disturbance of friable ACM of less than 10 ft^2 or 20 linear feet and associated with small repairs or maintenance.

-Licensed remover must notify MDE Air & Radiation Management Admin. (ARMA) in writing for project > O & M.
-Requires licensing for entity engaging in an asbestos project.
-Workers within preceding year must be medically examined to determine ability to wear a respirator.
-Specific sign requirements for > NESHAP with posting for 3 days prior to starting and placement outside of all entrances and exits. Must display startup and anticipated completion dates, posting date, and complaint information and phone number to ARMA.
-Specific air monitoring requirements of 1 per room and 1 per room size/volume.
-After cleaning and with barriers still up; send final written results to ARMA within 24 hours after receiving.
-Use of negative-pressure systems with at least 4 air changes per hour.
-Bag labeling to show license number, date of sealing, & where generated.
-Copy of disposal receipt or record of disposal to MDE within 10 days showing appropriate facility and date.
-Maintain records concerning each project for 6 years.
-Licensing application, fee, and revocation/suspension requirements.
-Safety & Health training course requirements.

COMAR 26.11.23

SCHOOL ASBESTOS ACCREDITATION OF INDIVIDUALS AND APPROVAL OF TRAINING COURSES

Updated in 1998

- **Applies to individuals performing asbestos projects in Maryland schools and public and commercial buildings and to persons applying for approval of training for asbestos occupations.**
- **Establishes training requirements for accreditation of specific types of disciplines for individuals working-with-asbestos.**
- **Requires a MD Photo ID card to work in MD**
- **Establishes fees for training providers' application.**
- **Establishes means to suspend or revoke a training course; and to decertify accredited persons.**

LABOR AND EMPLOYMENT ARTICLE
TITLE 5. OCCUPATIONAL SAFETY AND HEALTH
Subtitle 4.

ACCESS TO INFORMATION ABOUT HAZARDOUS AND TOXIC SUBSTANCES

Employer is required to generate and maintain a Chemical Information List (CIL) that lists the hazardous and toxic substances that an employee is exposed or potentially exposed.

Lists the chemicals alphabetically by common name, includes their chemicals name(s), and where it is found on the worksite.

Update every 2 years.

Copy sent to MDE initially and upon each updating.

Each employee has a right of access to the CIL within 1 day for viewing and 5 days for a copy.

COMAR 09.12.35
CONFINED SPACES

Applies only to construction work

Defines a confined space as a space:

(1) Having limited means of entry or egress;

(2) So enclosed that adequate dilution ventilation is not obtained by:
a. Natural air movement, or
b. Mechanically induced movement; and

(3) Subject to:
a. The accumulation of toxic or combustible agents, or
b. An oxygen deficiency

If determined to be a confined space:

(1) a blind or other device capable of ensuring complete closure must block lines entering the CS that contains a harmful agent.

(2) there must be Lock out/tag out (LOTO) on electrical service equipment.

(3) you must test the internal atmosphere for oxygen deficiency first, then test for the combustible gases and any other potential air contaminants.

(4) you must provide safe lighting, rescue equipment, employees trained in rescue procedures and CPR, and maintain constant communication with employees inside the CS, and have written emergency rescue procedures.

NOTE: There is a Federal OSHA Permit-Required Confined Spaces standard (29 CFR 1910.146) for General Industry operations. In an attempt to ascertain what standard applies, the COMAR regulation would apply if the work being done was a construction operation. Asbestos being removed from within a confined space would fall under the COMAR regulation. If an employee entered a utility/steam tunnel to turn off a valve, the permit-required standard would apply if it met that standard's confined space criteria requirements.

To be a permit-required confined space it must have one or more of the following characteristics: (1) contains or has the potential to contain a hazardous atmosphere, (2) contains a material that has the potential for engulfing an entrant, (3) has an internal configuration that might cause an entrant to be trapped or asphyxiated by inwardly converging walls or by a floor that slopes downward and tapers to a smaller cross section, and/or (4) contains any other recognized serious safety or health hazards.

DISCUSSION QUESTIONS

1. Why do the federal government and states both have laws about asbestos?
2. Is the legal limit for asbestos totally safe?
3. Why do you have to keep asbestos out of the air when you already have to wear a respirator and a suit?
4. What are some of the "rights" that an employee has under the state employees asbestos program?

CHAPTER 3

ASBESTOS DISEASES - PART 1

In this chapter you will learn:

About the diseases caused by asbestos.
How asbestos gets into your body.
When asbestos is dangerous.
How much asbestos can make you sick.
How long it takes to get sick from asbestos.
How your respiratory (breathing) system works.
The connections between asbestos, smoking, and disease.

ASBESTOS DISEASES

Asbestos can kill you. When you work with asbestos, you must work carefully. You are in this class to learn how to protect yourself and others from asbestos exposure. Asbestos exposure means breathing or swallowing asbestos fibers. If you are in an area where asbestos is in the air and you are not protected, then you are exposed. This is called asbestos exposure.

Asbestos exposure can cause:

Asbestosis (white lung): a disease that causes scars on the lungs.
Lung cancer: a cancer of the lungs.
Mesothelioma: a cancer of the lining of the chest or the lining of the abdomen.
Other cancers: cancers of the digestive system.

How do we know that asbestos can make you sick?

We know that asbestos causes asbestosis, mesothelioma, lung cancer, and other cancers because of many scientific studies. One of the most important studies looked at death certificates of union insulation workers who worked with asbestos. All of the men had worked with dangerous amounts of asbestos for at least 20 years. (This was before the OSHA standards).

These workers did not know how dangerous their work with asbestos was. No one told them that they needed to keep asbestos out of the air. No one told them that they had to protect themselves with respirators and disposable suits. There were no laws to protect them. Many of these workers died from asbestos disease.

Working with asbestos is a big responsibility

You are in this asbestos worker class for 4 days. You will learn that asbestos is dangerous. Asbestos can cause diseases that kill. You will learn when asbestos is most dangerous and how to keep the danger levels as low as possible. You will learn how to protect yourself, others, and the environment as you work with asbestos. Use the information from this class when you work. Ask for and use correctly the right equipment and protective gear. This will help to reduce the risk of getting an asbestos-related disease.

When is asbestos dangerous?

You cannot tell when you are breathing asbestos!

Asbestos is dangerous when it is in the air. When asbestos is in the air, you cannot see it, but you breathe it or swallow it. Asbestos is dangerous when it gets into your body. Asbestos gets into your body when you breathe or swallow it. Asbestos enters your body through your nose and mouth. Remember that asbestos fibers are so small you can' t see them. You cannot see, feel, or taste asbestos. Asbestos will not make you cough or sneeze. It will not make your throat or skin itch. Other materials mixed with the asbestos may cause these reactions however. Asbestos has no warning properties does not let you know it is there.

How much asbestos is dangerous?

There is no amount of asbestos that has proven to be safe!

The more asbestos you are exposed to, the more likely you are to get an asbestos-related disease. All of the asbestos diseases except one are **dose-related.** Dose-related means the more asbestos you breathe, the more likely you are to get an asbestos-related disease. You may not get sick until many years after you breathe the asbestos.

The more asbestos you breathe, the more likely you are to get asbestosis. The more asbestos you breathe, the more likely you are to get lung cancer. The more asbestos you breathe, the more likely you are to get a digestive system cancer. **Asbestosis, lung cancer, and digestive system cancers are dose-related.**

The asbestos-related disease that is different is mesothelioma. Small amounts of asbestos can give you mesothelioma. Asbestos workers' families have gotten mesothelioma from the dust the workers brought home on their clothes. Like other things that cause cancer, **there is no amount of asbestos that has been proven to be safe.**

How long does it take to get sick from asbestos?

Asbestos can make you sick 10 to 40 years after you breathe it. All of the asbestos diseases have a **latency period**. The **latency period** is the gap between the time you breathe asbestos and the time you start to feel sick. The latency period for asbestos diseases is approximately **ten and forty years** long. Even if you only worked with asbestos for a year and then stopped, you still might get sick ten to forty years later, depending on the amount of asbestos you were exposed to.

If you breathe tear gas, it will make you feel ill right away. It will make your eyes water and throat hurt as soon as you are exposed to it. **If you breathe asbestos, you probably won' t even know you are breathing it.** Asbestos does not irritate you while you are being exposed to it. It gives no warning. You will not feel sick during the latency period of ten to forty years. If you get an asbestos-related disease, you will begin to feel sick <u>after</u> the latency period.

Not everyone who is exposed to asbestos gets an asbestos-related disease. But anyone who is exposed to asbestos has a higher risk of getting an asbestos disease. Most of the asbestos related diseases are difficult to treat and to cure. The only cure for most asbestos diseases is to prevent them

Except for colon cancer, **asbestos diseases** - asbestosis, lung cancer, mesothelioma (a cancer) - **are very difficult to treat. The only cure for most asbestos diseases is to prevent them.**

When you breathe in asbestos, a few fibers are caught in your throat before they get to your lungs. But many **fibers lodge in your lungs, and stay there for the rest of your life.** It is important to stop these fibers from entering your lungs. You can keep many of these fibers out of your lungs with the safe work practices and personal protection you will learn about in this course.

How your lungs work.

To understand how asbestos makes you sick, you need to know how your respiratory (breathing) system works. Your respiratory system brings oxygen (a gas in the air) into your body. You cannot live without oxygen for more than a couple of minutes. When you breathe in, air, oxygen goes into your lungs. Your lungs are like a giant sponge with a huge surface area for taking in oxygen. **Your lungs take oxygen out of the air into your blood and get rid of carbon dioxide** (a waste gas in your blood). Then your heart pumps the oxygen rich blood through your body. Every cell in your body needs the oxygen that comes through your lungs.

Take a deep breath. When you breathe in, air goes through your nose and mouth into your windpipe. The windpipe divides into smaller and smaller tubes and finally ends in **tiny sacs called alveoli (al-VE-o-lie)**. In the alveoli, oxygen from the air goes into your blood and carbon dioxide from your blood goes through your lungs and out of your body when you breathe out. The alveoli are like the leaves on a tree. In the alveoli, oxygen passes into the blood and carbon dioxide waste goes out. The walls of your alveoli have to be very thin so that oxygen and carbon dioxide can move through them.

When you breathe, your chest moves in and out. It widens or expands when you breathe in, so that more air can come into your lungs. When you breathe out, your chest narrows or contracts, as your lungs push out the carbon dioxide. There is a two-layered lining called the **pleura**. It lines your lungs and rib cage. This lining lubricates your chest. It reduces the friction caused by breathing.

All of the parts of your respiratory system work together so that you can breathe and live.

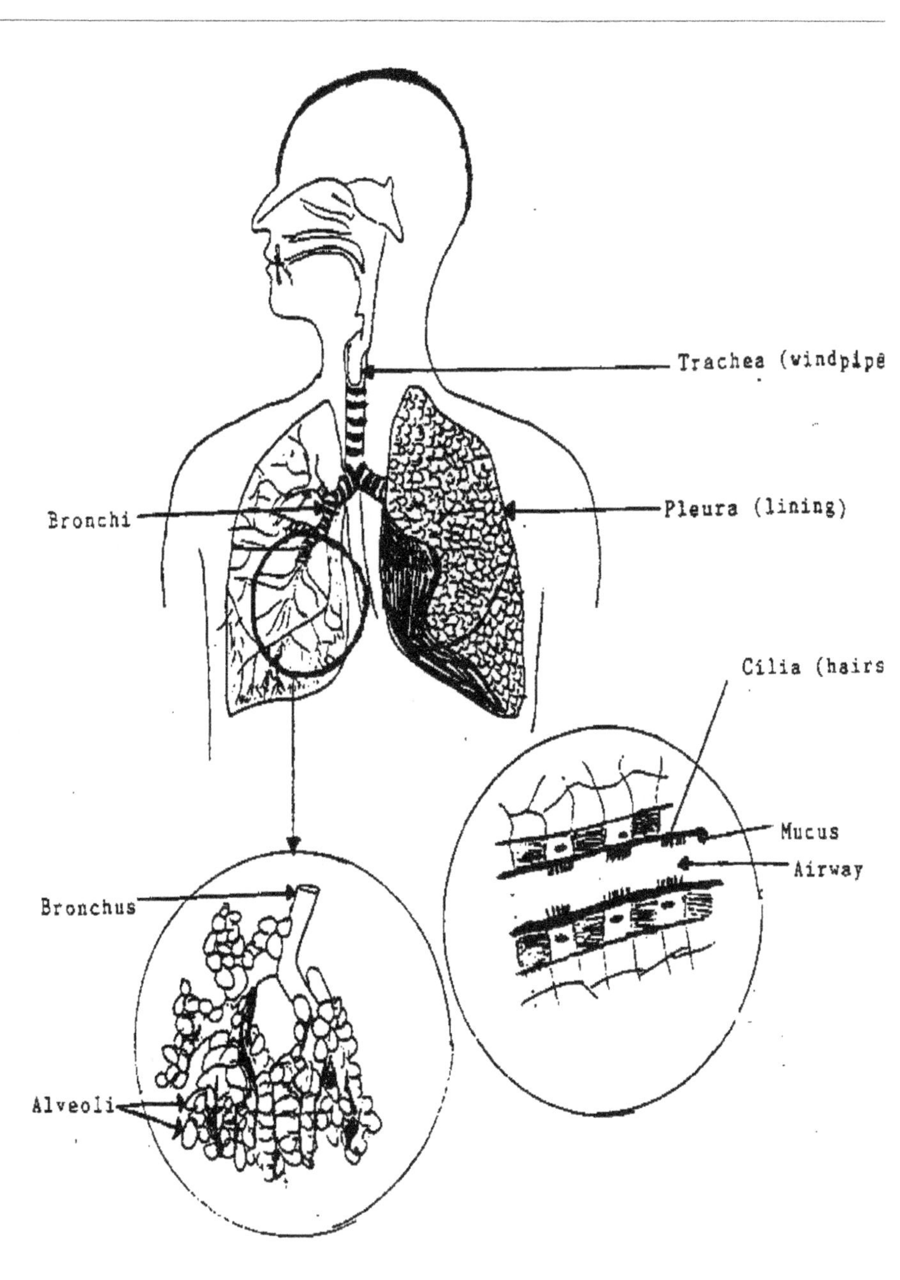
Trachea (windpipe
Bronchi
Pleura (lining)
Cilia (hairs
Mucus
Airway
Bronchus
Alveoli

Your body' s defenses against asbestos.

Your breathing (respiratory) system has some good defenses against breathing in dusts and fibers that can hurt you. **But the small asbestos fibers can overcome your body' s natural defenses and make you sick years later. Here are some of your body' s defenses against asbestos:**

Nose Hairs - dust and fibers get stuck in the hairs of your nose. You sneeze to get rid of it. You can blow out the large asbestos fibers. The smaller fibers travel on to your throat.

Muco-ciliary Escalator - the cells in your windpipe are covered with tiny hairs called cilia (Silly - uh). These tiny hairs beat in an upward motion. There are other cells in your windpipe that make mucus, a sticky gum - like substance. Some of the asbestos fibers stick to the mucus. The cilia wave upward, slowly pushing the fibers up to the back of your throat. Then you will either cough them out or swallow them. Cigarette smoke paralyzes the tiny hairs. It destroys one of your body' s important defenses againtsasbestos. You also swallow about a quart of mucus a day. If the mucus has asbestos fibers in it, then the fibers can lodge in your digestive system. Some of the smaller asbestos fibers travel into the branches of your breathing system. They then lodge in your lungs or the lining of your lungs. They may even enter your bloodstream.

White Blood Cells (Phagocytes) and Scar Formation - this part of your immune system tries to eat up asbestos, just like it would eat up a germ. But the asbestos fibers either kill or outlive the white blood cells. The dead cells wrap around the asbestos fibers and your body forms scar tissue. This scar tissue on your alveoli (air sacs) is called **fibrosis.** The scarring thickens the walls of the alveoli and makes it difficult for oxygen to reach the blood. This scarring can become asbestosis.

Diseases Caused by Asbestos		
Disease	**Signs & Symptoms**	**Treatment of Symptoms**
Asbestosis 10-20 yrs. to develop	Severely Short of Breath Dry Cough Feeling Very Tired Clubbed Fingers	Treatment, but no cure. Stop working with asbestos. Stop smoking Get flu shots Treat all chest colds quickly.
Lung Cancer 20-30 yrs. to develop	Short of Breath Constant Cough Feeling Tired and Weak Deep Chest Pain Cough up Blood Weight Loss	Treatments: surgery, radiation, chemotherapy. 9% to 13% live for 5 years or more. Poor cure rate. **Smoking multiplies your risk of getting lung cancer.** **STOP SMOKING!**
Mesothelioma 30-50 yrs. to develop	**Chest** (pleural): lodges in the lining of the chest. Short of breath. Dull chest pain under the ribs. Swelling in chest. **Belly** (peritoneal): lodges in the lining of the abdomen. Swollen stomach Belly pain Weight loss	No treatment, some medical procedures for pain reduction. Will kill you in 6 months to 2 years after it is discovered. A few people have lived up to 5 years.
Digestive System Cancers 20- 30 yrs.to develop	Change in bowel patterns Blood in bowel movement Feeling Tired Weight Loss	Treatment: Surgery, Radiation, and Chemotherapy. Chances of living good if colon cancer found early. 80% to 90% live for 5 years or more.

Asbestosis (as-bes-TO-sis) - a scarring of the lungs that can weaken and destroy your lungs ("white lung"). Asbestosis is not a cancer. It is a progressive disease. This means that scars keep forming in your lungs even after you stop asbestos exposure.

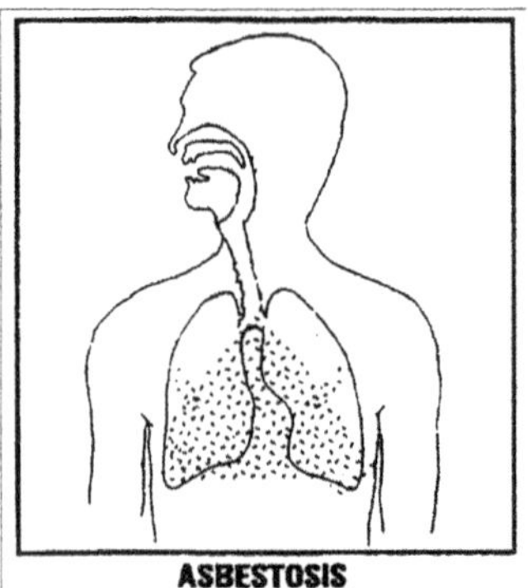
ASBESTOSIS

When you breathe in asbestos fibers, they go deep into your lungs. Asbestos fibers are skinny, sharp, and jagged. They lodge in your lungs like tiny needles. **Your body forms scars around them.** The scarred lungs cannot get oxygen into your blood any more. The scarred areas of your lungs become useless. You have to breathe more often to get the oxygen you need. You become short of breath. (See the chart on the previous page for other symptoms.)

When you have asbestosis, your heart (your body' s pump) has to work much harder to get blood with enough oxygen to all the cells of your body. Many people with asbestosis die from heart attacks or heart failure because their hearts are overworked. Other people with asbestosis die of pneumonia, other infections, and respiratory failure, because asbestosis weakens them.

Asbestosis is dose - related. The more asbestos you breathe, the more likely you are to get asbestosis. The more asbestos you breathe, the more severe the asbestosis will be.

What is cancer? Many cancers are linked to asbestos exposure. Cancer is a name for a large group of diseases, which affect many different parts of the body. All cancers are made up of cells, which are not normal. These abnormal cancer cells grow rapidly out of control. They either remain in one area of the body and form a tumor or they spread to other areas of the body where they cause harm.

Mesothelioma (mes-o-the-lee-O-ma) - a rare but deadly cancer - It is the different asbestos disease. Low levels of asbestos exposure can cause mesothelioma. It is estimated that less than 2% of asbestos worker deaths are caused by mesothelioma. Mesothelioma is a difficult disease to identify or diagnose. It is often not identified or is misdiagnosed. It is difficult to know how rare this disease really is.

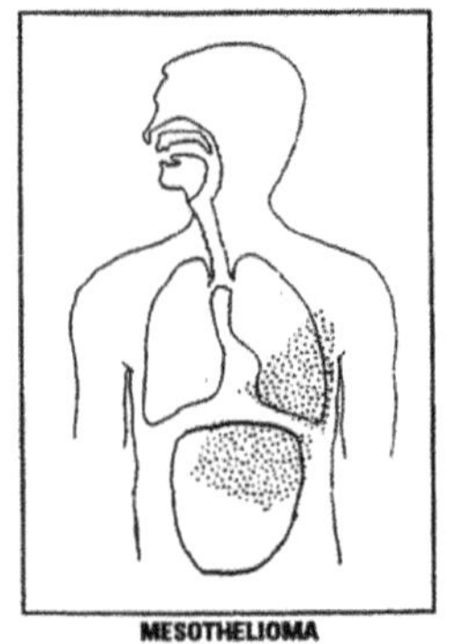
MESOTHELIOMA

There are two types of mesothelioma:

(1) **Pleural mesothelioma** is a cancer that attacks the 2-layered pleural lining of the chest.

(2) **Peritoneal mesothelioma** is a cancer that attacks the lining of the abdomen (belly).

Most of the time mesothelioma is caused by exposure to asbestos. Because of this, it is called a "marker" disease. This means that if someone has mesothelioma, it is highly likely that they have been exposed to asbestos. Mesothelioma has been directly linked to asbestos exposure in at least 96% of the documented cases. There is no cure or effective treatment for mesothelioma. It kills most people 6 months to 2 years after it is detected. Some people have lived as long as 5 years after their mesothelioma was discovered.

Mesothelioma has the longest latency period of all the asbestos diseases. The latency period for mesothelioma is between 30 and 50 years. Children are the exception to the long latency period rule. A child' s body grows at a rapid rate. The latency period for a child is much shorter than for an adult.

It may only take a very small amount of asbestos to give you mesothelioma. Mesothelioma has killed asbestos worker' s wives, children, and even pet dogs. This is why you must not take asbestos home with you on your clothes. We say that mesothelioma is **NOT dose-related** because low levels of asbestos exposure can cause this disease.

There is no amount of asbestos that has been proven to be safe.

Lung cancer

Smoking multiplies your chances of getting lung cancer.

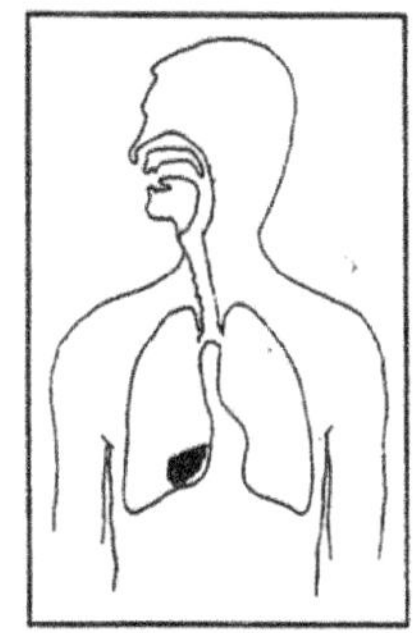

LUNG CANCER

Asbestos is a strong cancer - causing substance. **Lung cancer is the biggest killer of all the asbestos diseases. Between 20% and 25% of asbestos worker deaths are caused by lung cancer.** Lung cancer is cancer that develops in the lung. It is dose related.

Asbestos and smoking together are a deadly mix. The risk of getting lung cancer is not just the risk from smoking plus the risk from asbestos. It is the risk from smoking times the risk from asbestos!

Prevent lung cancer: quit smoking and avoid exposure!

What does all this mean?

Lung cancer has the highest death rate of all the asbestos diseases.

An asbestos worker **who does not smoke** is about 5 times more likely to get lung cancer than someone who does not work with asbestos.

A smoker **who does not work with asbestos is** about 10 to 22 times more likely than a non-smoker to get lung cancer. So if all you did was smoke and never worked with asbestos, your risk of lung cancer would be 4 times more than an asbestos worker who never smoked.

But, when you combine smoking and asbestos exposure, the **combination** is **deadly**. **Asbestos workers who smoke are about 50 to 90 times more likely to get lung cancer.** Lung cancer is a horrible disease. Your probability of a cure is only 11%. It is a disease that drains you and your loved ones emotionally and financially for a long time. The best thing you can do is to prevent this disease. **Quit smoking and avoid asbestos exposure.**

If you are a smoker, get help to quit. Nicotine addiction and the pleasure of smoking make smoking a very difficult habit to break. How difficult a habit (or addiction) is to break can be measured. It is measured by the percent of relapse. Relapse means that you tried to stop smoking, but started again. Let' s say you stopped smoking for 30 days. Then on day 31, you picked up a cigarette and by day 40 you were smoking a pack a day again. You just had a relapse. About 70% of smokers who quit, relapse in the first three months. The rate of relapse is about the same for those who are addicted to heroin and those who are alcoholics.

There is hope. Surveys show that most people who keep trying to quit finally succeed. There are many programs that can help you stop smoking. Please get help. Your local chapter of the American Lung Association can give you a list of where you can go to get help.

Other cancers

Many other cancers are more often found in asbestos workers then in people who don' t work with asbestos. These cancers include cancers of the digestive system, i.e. cancer in the mouth, the esophagus (the tube from your mouth to your stomach), the stomach, and the lower intestine (colon and rectum). A doctor may be able to successfully treat colon and rectum cancer **if the doctor finds it early.** Digestive system cancers are **dose -related.**

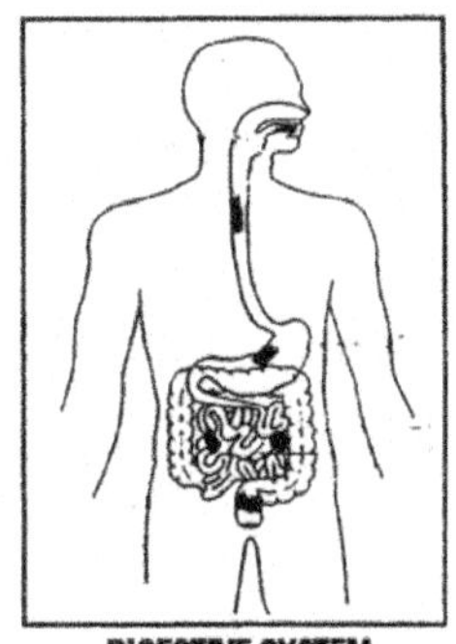

DIGESTIVE SYSTEM CANCER

Other Signs of Asbestos Exposure

Pleural Plaques are found in asbestos workers. They are lesions that grow slowly. They are made of fibrous tissue that can harden. They are found in the lining of the lungs. You may not even know you have pleural plaques until you get a chest X-ray. You may never have a problem with them. Always alert your doctor about them. If you have these plaques, your risk of lung cancer doubles. You may also develop asbestosis, which is a scarring of the lining of the lungs. Smoking does not cause Pleural plaques.

Pleural Effusion is fluid between the chest wall and the lungs.

Pleural Thickening is a thickening of the lining of the chest or lung cavity.

Asbestos Bodies are asbestos fibers that have been encapsulated by your body. They are found when a doctor takes a sample of lung tissue, stains it, and looks at it under a microscope.

Asbestos Warts are skin lesions caused by asbestos irritation. They are generally associated with higher levels of asbestos exposure. Asbestos is not known to enter the body through the skin

If you protect yourself and keep asbestos out of the air, you lower your odds of getting sick!

ASBESTOS DISEASES

Key Facts

Asbestos can kill you unless you protect yourself

Asbestos is silent and deadly. You do not know it is there because the fibers are so small. You cannot see, hear, feel, taste, smell or sense the small asbestos fibers that enter your body.

When asbestos is in the air, it gets into your body when you breathe and when you swallow.

Diseases

Asbestos causes four types of disease:

1. Asbestosis, "white lung" - a scarring of the lungs, which makes it hard to breath.
2. Mesothelioma, the "marker disease" - a cancer of the lining of the lungs or the lining of the belly. It is rare but it always kills. It is not dose-related.
3. Lung Cancer (also caused by smoking) is the biggest killer of all the asbestos diseases. **Asbestos workers who smoke are 50 to 90 times more likely to get lung cancer then the general public.**
4. Other Cancers - cancers of the belly or gut.

Dose-related

The more asbestos fibers you breathe or swallow, the more likely you are to get sick. This is called a dose relationship. The higher the amount of asbestos, the greater your chances of getting an asbestos disease. Mesothelioma is the exception.

Latency period

All of the asbestos diseases have a latency period. The latency period is the time gap between when you take the asbestos into your body and when you become sick. For asbestos diseases the latency period is between 10 and 40 years long.

Discussion questions

1. Why is it important to know about the health hazards of asbestos?
2. When is asbestos dangerous?
3. Is there a safe level of asbestos exposure?
4. How do we know that asbestos causes diseases that can kill?

For more information

*OSHA Asbestos Standard, 29 CFR 1926.1101.

American Lung Association

White Lung Association

Sourcebook on Asbestos Diseases, George A. Peters and Barbara J. Peters, Garland STPM Press, 1980.

Asbestos Disease Update, George A. Peters and Barbara J. Peters, Garland Publishing, 1989.

Asbestiform Fibers: Nonoccupational Health Risks, National Research Council, National Academy Press, 1984.

***Your instructor may have a copy of this publication for you to look at.**

Asbestos diseases exercise

This is not a test. It is an exercise. Use it to see for yourself how well you understand the material in the chapter?

1. How do asbestos fibers enter your body?

2. What is a latency period?

3. What does dose-related mean?

4. What are the diseases that asbestos causes?

5. How do asbestos exposure and smoking cigarettes mix?

ASBESTOS DISEASES -Part 2: Medical Exams

In this chapter you will learn:

What happens during a medical exam.
Why you need a medical exam.
When to have a medical exam.
About the medical records your employer has to keep.

MEDICAL EXAMS

A doctor can help you find medical problems early.

If you work with asbestos, you must have a special kind of medical exam called **medical surveillance (medical monitoring).** You have to have a medical exam before you start work and once a year thereafter. The doctor who gives you medical surveillance is a doctor whose specialty is **occupational diseases.** Your occupation or job causes occupational diseases. Asbestos causes occupational disease. Medical exams may be required by State and OSHA law under certain conditions.

You must have a **baseline** exam before you start to work. The baseline exam documents your current health condition and your fitness for duty (including your ability to wear a respirator). It is the first medical exam that you get with the job. It is a long and complete exam that usually takes 2-3 hours.

Each year after that you have a follow-up medical exam. The doctor looks for any changes in your health since your first exam. With the yearly exam, a disease can be found early. The earlier an asbestos disease is found the better your chances for treatment. Be sure to get these exams. They can save your life. Your Agency pays for these exams.

Initial asbestos medical exams will have at least these four parts:

1. **A work/medical history,** to see if you' ve ever worked with materials that might have damaged your lungs. These include coal dust, cotton fibers, silica or asbestos. This is a long **questionnaire.** It asks you about what kind of work you' ve done in the past. It asks you about your smoking habits. It asks you about any lung diseases you have had. In addition, there will be questions about respirator and protective equipment usage.

DOCTOR TAKING WORK HISTORY

There are certain questions on the questionnaire that OSHA requires. These questions must be asked. The employer must include these questions on the questionnaire. He or she cannot substitute his/her own. The questionnaire is about 20 pages long.

2. **A general physical exam** that concentrates on your lungs, heart, and stomach. This is to see if your lungs, heart, and stomach are normal and in good shape. In your baseline exam, the doctor will document your health **and state how healthy you are before you work with asbestos.** It is also to make sure that you don' t have any medical problems that asbestos exposure would make worse. After checking your lungs and heart, the doctor will tell if you can wear a respirator (a mask that protects you from asbestos,) and if you can work with asbestos.

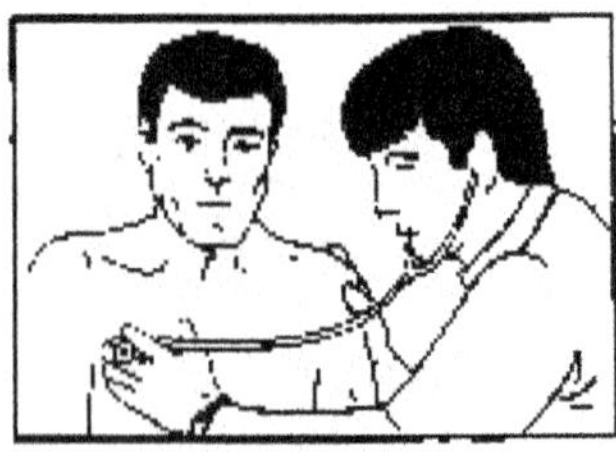

GENERAL PHYSICAL EXAM

In the yearly exam, the doctor looks for any signs (symptoms) of asbestosis, lung cancer, or other asbestos diseases. For example, the doctor will listen for "rales"or crackling sounds in your lungs, which may be a sign that you are getting asbestosis.

3. A breathing test, called a **Pulmonary Function Test** (PFT). A breathing test makes sure that your lungs are **not** damaged before you begin work. It is used as a comparison for later tests. You blow out through a tube using your mouth. Your nose is held shut so that you do not breathe through it. All the air that your lungs push out is measured. A meter reads how much air you can blow out in one second. The breathing test is a very simple, safe test. This test often gives the first clue that your lungs are being hurt by asbestos.

PULMONARY FUNCTION TEST

Remember, it is important to find and manage asbestos diseases early. Smoking, a heavy meal, or a bad cold may also result in poor pulmonary function test results.

4. A **chest x-ray** to make sure that your lungs are not damaged before you begin to work. It is compared to future x-rays to find any changes that take place in your lungs as you work with asbestos over the years. The need for a chest x-ray is based on your doctor' s decision. It is usually part of the baseline examination.

   The x-ray must be checked by a doctor with experience in reading x-rays of **work-related** lung diseases. Doctors who are trained and certified to read x-rays for asbestos workers are called **"B readers".**

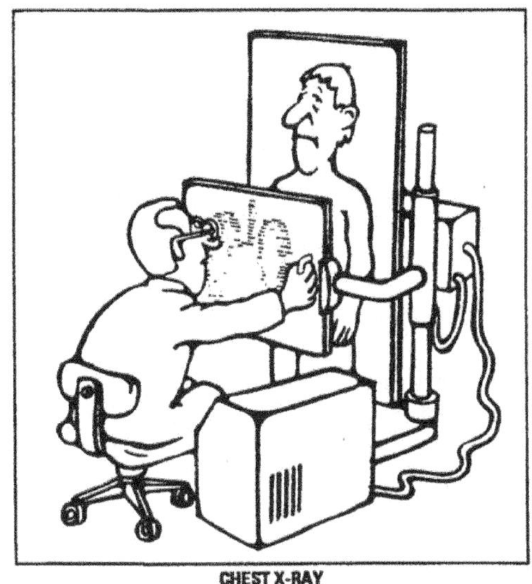
CHEST X-RAY

Additional tests may be ordered at the doctor's discretion.

When must workers have medical exams?

You must have a medical exam before you start Level II work and then:

The Maryland State Employees Asbestos Program will provide exams annually thereafter as well as give you one when you leave State service.

For Non-Level II employees **working in the State of Maryland**, the COMAR law says that medical exams are required before any asbestos work begins.

For Non-Level II employees elsewhere, the OSHA law says that your employer must provide medical exams.

1. **Medical exams are required whenever you are engaged in Class I, II, or III asbestos work more than 30 days per year as defined in the OSHA Asbestos Standard.** You will learn about these classes of work in later sections of this manual.

2. **Medical exams are required whenever you are exposed to asbestos above the permissible exposure or excursion limits. The permissible exposure limit is 0.1 fibers per cubic centimeter.** At the Permissible Exposure Level, the average number of fibers sampled over an eight-hour period is 0.1 f/cc. **The excursion Limit is 1**

fiber per cubic centimeter (f/cc). The Excursion Limit of 1 f/cc is the average number of fibers sampled over a 30-minute period.

3. **Medical exams are required whenever you must wear a negative pressure respirator.** You will learn about negative pressure respirators in the next section. A doctor must medically clear you before you can wear a respirator. This is to make sure that your heart and lungs can handle the strain of wearing a respirator.

Why are medical exams required?

Yearly medical exams are the quickest way to tell if asbestos is making you sick. The exams are for finding asbestos diseases early and to make sure that you can safely wear a respirator. Remember that most asbestos-related diseases get worse, the more asbestos you breathe. It' s important to find these diseases as early as possible so that treatment will be more effective. Medical exams are used as evidence for Workers' Compensation. Workers' Compensation is a no-fault insurance system. You must prove that you got your disease or injury on the job. Medical exams also help doctors do research on asbestos diseases, so we can prevent them in the future.

The first exam shows a baseline - how healthy you were when you started work. **Yearly exams can catch a problem when it first starts.** The yearly exam is a little shorter than the first one. It also includes 3 to 4 parts:

1. A questionnaire every year. This is also an official OSHA (Occupational Safety & Health Administration) questionnaire. It asks about your work experience, smoking habits, and lung diseases over the past year.

2. A general physical exam each year, just like the first year.

3. Pulmonary Function Test (PFT' s) each year, just lie the first year.

4. A chest X-ray every 5 years (more often if you' re older and /or have worked with asbestos for more than 10 years, less often if the doctor says so). You do not <u>need</u> to have a chest X-ray every year. The table below is a recommended (not required) schedule. The examining physician will also use his/her professional judgment when deciding the need for a chest x-ray.

RECOMMENDED SCHEDULE FOR CHEST X-RAYS			
Years Since First Worked With Asbestos	**Age Now 18 - 35**	**Age Now 36 - 45**	**Age Now Over 45**
0 to 10 Years	Every 5 Years	Every 5 Years	Every 5 Years
More Than 10 Years	Every 5 years	Every 2 Years	Once A Year

Many people' s lives have been saved by these tests. Employers are required by OSHA law to provide these tests for their workers. The tests are not to punish you for getting sick on the job. They are to keep you from getting sicker if asbestos begins to make you sick. Medical surveillance however, is not prevention. Once an asbestos-related disease is found, the person has that disease. Thus, it is extremely important to follow safe work practices and wear appropriate protective equipment. The earlier most asbestos diseases are found the better your chances for treatment. Medical exams are also very important if you ever have to file for workers' compensation or disability.

After these medical exams, the doctor writes a confidential report and must send a copy to you at your home address. **The doctor only tells your employer whether you are able to wear a respirator or not and if there are any limitations on your work.**

Your employer pays for the doctor. The law requires the employer to inform the doctor of the **required** and recommended tests for the medical exam. The employer must also inform the doctor not to report any findings that are not related to your ability to wear a respirator or work with asbestos. You are the doctor' s patient. By law, the doctor must not tell your employer anything about your health unless it will prevent you from doing asbestos work. **You must be given a copy of the doctor' s report within 30 days after getting the exam.**

RECORDS

Your employer must keep your medical records for 30 years after you leave the job

You have the right to get copies of your medical records from the doctor. You may want the information from your medical records 20 - 30 years from now. **YOU MAY WISH TO GET A COPY OF YOUR ENTIRE MEDICAL RECORD AND KEEP IT IN A SAFE PLACE.** A safe deposit box is a good place to keep them. Thirty years from now, you may need these records, and they need to be in a place where you can find them.

If you wish to obtain a copy of your medical records for yourself or wish a copy to go to a designated representative, you must call the State Employees Asbestos Program office to obtain a medical release form to be presented to the clinic.

Beyond medical exams

There are some things you can do to lower your risk of getting a disease from working with asbestos:

1. **Always remember how dangerous asbestos can be.**
   The law requires your employer to give you the right equipment and protective gear but you need to do a good job using the equipment and protective gear. Following the safe work practices that you learn in this course protects you and everyone else around you. Keep asbestos out of the air. Use the right equipment. Work safely. Protect yourself with the right respirator and disposable suit.

2. **Quit smoking.** There are many places you can go for help to quit smoking. Encourage others to quit smoking.

3. **Inform any doctor you visit that you have worked with asbestos.** Tell the doctor the year when you started working with asbestos. Tell the doctor how long you worked with it. Asbestos diseases have a latency period of ten to forty years. Tell the doctor about all the diseases that asbestos causes and ask the doctor to look for those diseases.

4. **Even after you stop working with asbestos, you should have a yearly exam.** (At this time the State Employees Asbestos Program will provide these for you if you request them). This is even more important if you worked with asbestos over 10 years ago.

5. **You have the right to know what you are working with.** Work with your agency, co-workers, and union, to ensure that you get the information that you need.

MEDICAL EXAMS

Key Facts

Asbestos workers have to have medical surveillance, a special kind of doctor' s checkup:

1. before they start work,
2. once a year

Medical exams are the quickest way to tell if asbestos is making you sick.

A medical exam includes:

First Exam (baseline)

- Long questionnaire
- General physical (lung, heart, stomach)
- Lung test [Pulmonary Function Test (PFT)]
- Chest X-ray

Every Year (follow-up)

- Short questionnaire
- General physical
- Lung test (PFT)
- Chest X-ray at the discretion of the physician

Your employer must ensure that you get a copy of the results of your medical exam within 30 days after the exam.

Your employer must keep your medical records for over 30 years.

Discussion questions

1. What good is medical surveillance?
2. Why is it important to find asbestos diseases early?
3. Why is it important to have an asbestos medical exam before doing any asbestos work?
4. When are medical exams required?
5. List the required parts of an asbestos medical exam.
6. What is the baseline exam?
7. How long must the employer keep the medical records?
8. Why keep copies of your medical records?
9. What do I do when I am no longer working with asbestos and do not get yearly medical surveillance?

For more information

*OSHA Asbestos Standard, 29 CFR 1926.1101.

Stop smoking Information:

Call your local chapter of the American Lung Association

Call your local chapter of the American Cancer Society

Look under the yellow pages under "Smoking".

***Your instructor may have a copy of this publication for you to look at.**

RESPIRATORS - Part 1: Types

In this chapter you will learn:

- **What respirators are.**
- **You must wear a respirator when you work with asbestos.**
- **How respirators work.**
- **Respirators are not perfect.**
- **Respirators have to fit.**
- **Not everyone can wear a respirator.**
- **What kinds of respirators are allowed on an asbestos job.**
- **What kinds of respirators are not allowed on an asbestos job.**
- **How to figure out whether you have the right respirator for the job.**

What is a respirator?

Respirators are your last line of defense against asbestos.

You need to keep asbestos out of the air when you work with it. One way to do this is to keep asbestos wet and use other control methods outlined in this course. But no matter what you do, some asbestos will still be in the air. This is why **you have to wear a respirator.** A respirator is a device that a person wears that filters the air in the work area or supplies clean air from outside the work room. The purpose of a respirator is to provide clean, breathable, air to the user.

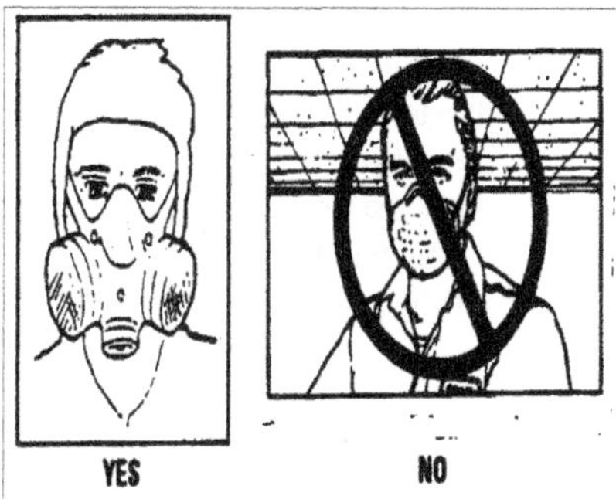

Paper dust masks will not protect anyone from asbestos. They are illegal on asbestos jobs.

Use only NIOSH approved respirators for asbestos.

THE LAST LINE OF DEFENSE

Respirators are your last line of defense. They are absolutely necessary to protect your lungs from asbestos disease. Workers don' t like respirators. Respirators are uncomfortable, hot, and heavy. They block your sight, and they make it harder to breathe. It is important to remember why you have to wear these uncomfortable pieces of equipment. Remember you are protecting yourself from asbestos diseases by wearing them.

Respirators are also not a quick fix, though many people think they are. The State Employees Asbestos Program says that before they can wear a respirator, workers have to have a doctor' s permission, a fitting session (called a fit test), and training. Respirators must be maintained and kept in good condition all the time. **Employers must also have a written respiratory protection program. They must do regular inspections to be sure that respirators actually protect workers and that the written program is meeting its stated objectives.**

A respirator is only as good as its fit

If you wear a respirator that doesn't fit, air and asbestos will leak in around the sides of the facepiece. Instead of being caught by the filters, asbestos will go into your lungs. This is why **the law says you must have a fit test.** The test tells whether the respirator seals around your face. A respirator that does not fit looks the same as one that does. There is no way to tell if a respirator protects you or not just by looking at it.

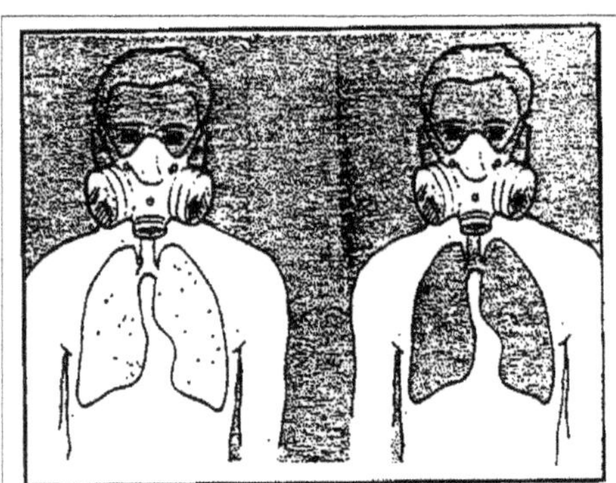

YOU CAN'T TELL BY LOOKING WHETHER A RESPIRATOR FITS OR NOT

NOT EVERYONE CAN WEAR A RESPIRATOR

Some people cannot find a respirator to fit their face. If you have a beard, you cannot wear any of the respirators approved for this program, even if it just a "5 o' clock shadow". If you have any hair on your face where the respirator seals, the respirator will not protect you. Even a large mustache can break the seal of your respirator.

If you have a broken nose you may not be able to wear a respirator. If you have missing teeth, large scars, a very narrow or broad face, or any face with an unusual shape you may not be able to wear a respirator. If you feel very anxious, a little faint and shaky when you first try a respirator on, you may not be able to wear a respirator. You may have claustrophobia, a fear of closed in spaces.

Respirators also make it harder for you to breathe. You have to have a medical checkup to be sure that your lungs and heart are strong enough to take the strain of working with a respirator. You must have permission from a doctor before you can wear a respirator on the job.

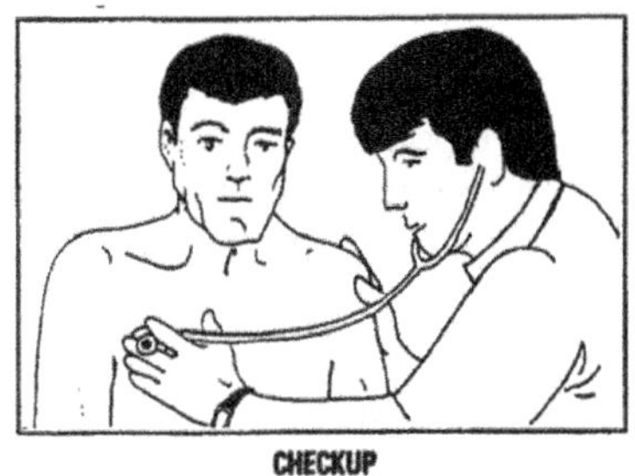

CHECKUP

When do you wear a respirator?

You must wear a respirator whenever you work with asbestos.

Asbestos is measured in fibers per cubic centimeter (f/cc) of air. A cubic centimeter is about the size of a sugar cube. One thousand cubic centimeters equal one liter, which is about the size of a quart. You breathe about one thousand liters of air every hour when you are working.

The State Employees Asbestos Program says that you have to wear a respirator under the following circumstances:

1. **Whenever you cut, break, or otherwise disturb asbestos.**
2. **When there is the possibility you might disturb asbestos during your work.**
3. **When you must work in an area where asbestos is being disturbed.**
4. **When you must enter a restricted area.**

NO RESPIRATOR IS PERFECT

Every kind of respirator has its good and bad points. Every respirator leaks. Some respirators protect you more than others. Each respirator described below has a protection factor (PF). This number tells you how much the respirator protects you.

The more asbestos in the air, the more you will need a respirator with greater protection

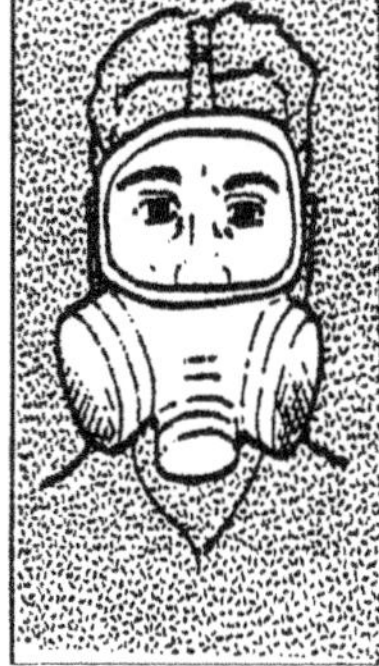

There are two kinds of respirators allowed on Level II asbestos jobs. Which respirator you wear depends on the amount of asbestos in the air and the working conditions. **Your employer must monitor a worker' s breathing air and working conditions.** Then he or she decides what kind of respirator is needed, based on how much asbestos is in air and what the working conditions are.

Respirators fall into two categories:

Air purifying respirators use a filter to clean (purify) the air that' s in the workplace.

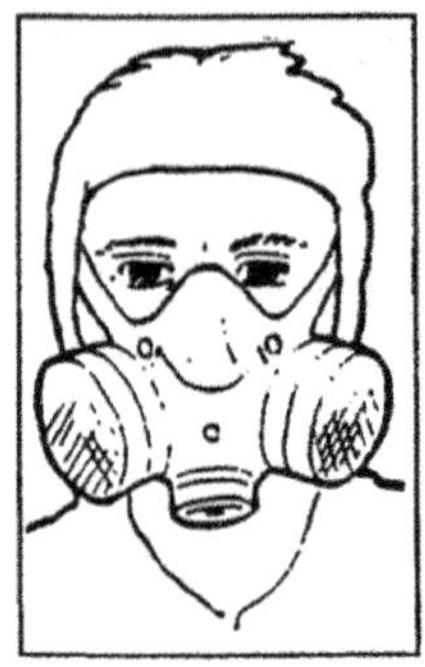

Air supplied respirators supply clean air to you from a compressor or air tanks, from a clean area outside the workplace.

Of the two kinds of respirators that you can use, one is an air purifying and the other is an air supplied.

RESPIRATORS APPROVED FOR USE BY STATE EMPLOYEES:

#1 POWERED AIR PURIFYING RESPIRATOR

This respirator is legal up to 100x the permissible exposure limit (PEL) of 0.1f/cc of asbestos. This means that the air can contain up to 10 f/cc of asbestos and it is still OK for you to use this respirator (**provided the motor is running properly**). This respirator has a facepiece that covers the entire face. It is attached to a motor. It has filters. The motor and filters can be worn either at your waist or face depending on the brand of respirator you have. The batteries are worn at the waist. The motor pulls air through the filters. If the motor is not attached to the facepiece, the air gets to the facepiece through a hose.

This respirator only filters the air that is already in the room. They cannot be used in atmosphere which area **IDLH (Immediately Dangerous to Life or Health).** It is an air-purifying respirator. Because it has a motor, this respirator is called a powered air purifying respirator or PAPR.

The air coming to the facepiece pushes air and asbestos away from the sides of the facepiece if leakage occurs. The motor makes a positive pressure inside the facepiece. One good thing about this type of respirator is that if it leaks, it leaks out. Another good thing about a powered air-purifying respirator (PAPR) is that your lungs do not have to work as hard to pull air through the filters. The motor does some of the work for you.

If the batteries are low or the motor isn't on, however, then this respirator is no better than a full-faced non-powered air-purifying respirator. Another problem with a PAPR is that it only filters the dirty air in the room. It is just like any other air-purifying respirator. If the batteries in the motor are run down, air and asbestos can leak in around the sides of the mask and cause exposure. This can also happen if the filters are clogged with dust or you breathe very hard. To reduce the risk of this happening, there are two things you must do. First of all make sure that you **flow test the PAPR before each use.** Flow testing lets you know if the filters are getting clogged or if the blower is blowing air at the proper flow rate (usually 4-6cfm/min.) Secondly make sure that the batteries are fully charged before every use. Also, run the batteries all the way down about once a month so they do not develop a "memory". (This means that an 8 hour battery may only run for 2 hours even when it is fully charged because it has only been used for periods of less than 8 hours over many months so it will no longer hold for more than this.) Newer nickel metal hydride batteries have overcome this problem and will not develop a memory.

Another concern is that of the HEPA filters on the respirator becoming overloaded and reducing the airflow too less than the minimum airflow requirement for the respirator (4 cfm or manufacturers requirement). Also when filters become overloaded this can lead to possibly tripping a circuit breaker on the battery pack. To avoid this problem change the HEPA filters as soon as a resistance in breathing is felt or when they become wet.

The motor on a PAPR blows air at the same rate no matter how hard you breathe. If you breathe very hard, it makes a suction or negative pressure inside the facepiece. The facepiece has to fit perfectly on your face. If it does not form an airtight seal, air and asbestos will leak in around the edges of the facepiece. This is called **over breathing** the respirator.

#1 POWERED AIR-PURIFYING RESPIRATOR (PAPR)

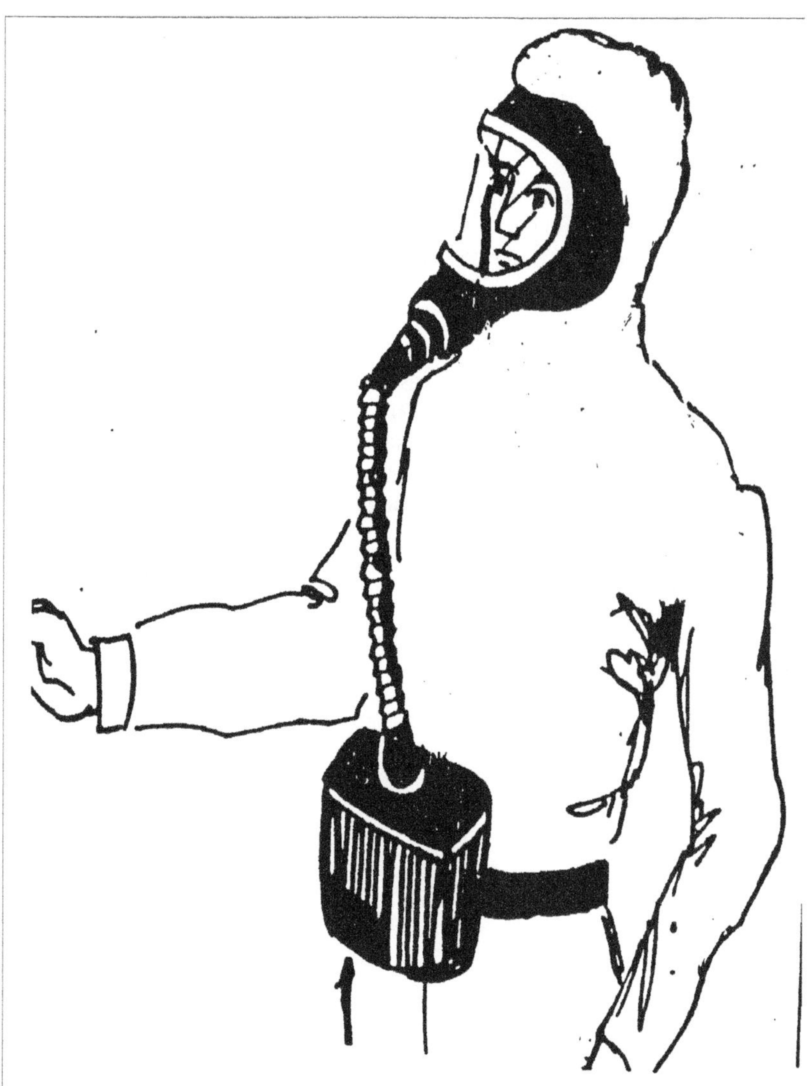

Protection Factor = 100 means: for every 100 fibers of asbestos outside the mask, only 1 fiber will leak in.

#2 PRESSURE-DEMAND AIR-SUPPLIED RESPIRATOR

This respirator can be used in air that contains up to one thousand times the PEL. This means the air can contain 100f/cc of asbestos and it is still OK for you to use this respirator. Fresh air comes in through a hose from another air source. It is a Type C supplied respirator. It is also a positive pressure respirator. One good thing about a positive pressure respirator is that if it leaks, clean air leaks out.

This respirator has a tiny valve, which gives you more air when you breathe harder. It is called a pressure demand respirator. When you breathe harder, more air comes through the hose into the face piece. A pressure demand respirator is the most protective of the respirators that you can use.

One problem with this type of respirator is that you can trip on the hose, or it can get caught on a scaffold. This type of respirator also has a limited range. The length of hose from the air source to the regulator is limited by law to 300 feet. The respirator needs an extra filter or, in the case of an area where the air contaminants may become immediately dangerous to life or health, a bottle of air (reserve air) in case the air supply is cut off. **Immediately Dangerous to Life or Health means that the air contaminants will injure or even kill you very quickly.**

#2 TYPE C PRESSURE-DEMAND AIR-SUPPLIED RESPIRATOR

protection factor = 1,000 legal up to 100 f/cc

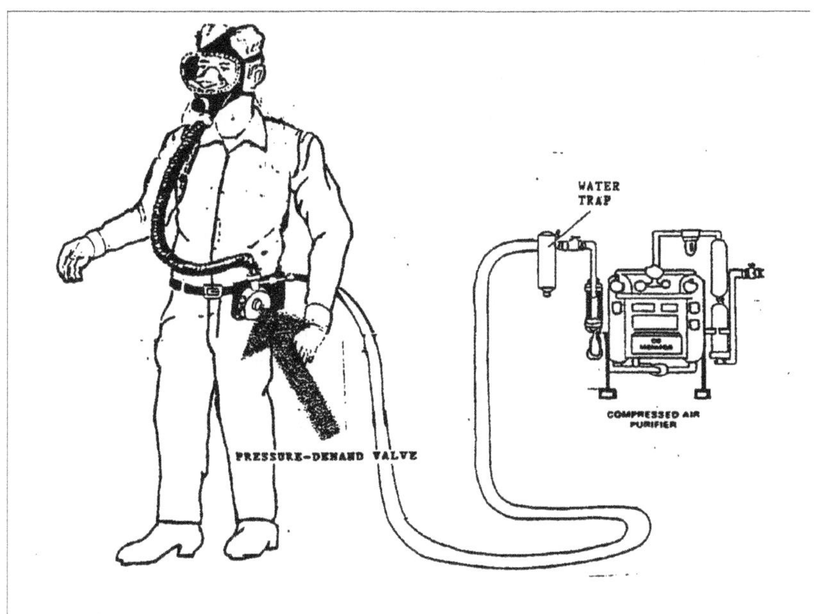

Protection Factor = 1000 means: for every 1000 asbestos fibers outside the mask, only 1 fiber will leak in.

MORE ABOUT TYPE C RESPIRATORS

Type C respirators are more complicated than other types of respirators. Fresh air must be supplied by either air tanks or a compressor. It is then supplied to the face piece through a hose. The air has to be clean, cool, and at low pressure so that it' s comfortable to breathe.

The air you breathe in a Type C respirator is called **"Grade D Air" or breathable air.** (You do not breathe pure oxygen in a Type C respirator). Grade D air is air that has19.5% to 23.5% oxygen in it. The hydrocarbons in it are < 5 Mil per cubic meter of air. It Grade D air also has 10ppm or less of carbon monoxide and 1000 ppm or less of carbon dioxide. There is no noticeable odor.

Carbon monoxide is a dangerous gas, which you can' t smell.

Your employer may use a special rig, which filters the air to Grade D quality. The source of air is supplied by a device called a compressor. He may also buy bottled air which the manufacturer or distributor certifies to be Grade D or "breathable".

If your employer chooses to use a compressor, it must not be a regular shop compressor. A regular compressor will pump dirty air into your mask. A compressor that is used to supply Grade D air must have these features:

1. **A filter to take out odors, dust and some chemicals.**
2. **A carbon monoxide (CO) alarm <u>or</u> a high temperature alarm. CO can come from compressors, which work at high temperatures, space heaters, forklifts, gas hot water heaters or from the outside air because of cars or trucks. A carbon monoxide alarm is better than a high temperature alarm.**
3. **A trap to catch water condensate or oil mists *(if using an oil lubricated compressor) in the air.**

***Oil-less compressors are strongly recommended**

The filters on the air purification panel must be cleaned and maintained in accordance with the manufacturer's requirements.

.

If the carbon monoxide alarm goes off, stop work immediately. Leave the area immediately. Supervisors must make sure all workers are out. They must make sure that all personnel using the respirators are accounted for.

TYPE OF SYSTEM	PRESSURE RANGE	RESERVE AIR
Low-pressure	100-200 psi*	has standby reserve air tanks
High-pressure	2000-4000 psi	has in-line, high-pressure tanks
*psi = pounds per square inch		

You may have up to 300 feet of hose for a Type C respirator. It is illegal to have more than 300 feet of hose with a Type C respirator.

IMPORTANT CONSIDERATIONS WITH TYPE C RESPIRATOR SYSTEMS

Training

Special training must be given to each worker who is using a Type C respirator. The training should be specific to the exact type of respirator that is issued. Supplied air respirators do not necessarily have emergency escape provisions. A HEPA filter or a small auxiliary escape tank of air attached & connected to the respirator can give you this safe escape mechanism. **In cases where the atmosphere in the work area may become immediately dangerous to life or health, only the auxiliary tank of air can be used for escape. The bottle of air must allow for 5 to 15 min. of air for escape.** If the atmosphere is already immediately dangerous to life or health you can' t use this respirator.

You must know how to use your escape gear. Remember, if the air you breathe is supplied, anything can happen to that air supply. When the source of your air is gone you will panic. It is very important to practice how to use your escape gear. If you practice, you are more likely to remember how to use your escape air when you need it.

A supervisor must watch the system

Type C respirator systems protect workers the most. They are also the most complicated respirator systems. There are individual respirators, many long hoses, manifolds, compressors, air tanks, pumps, and alarms. Each person using the Type C respirator should be aware of all the parts of the system and know how they operate.

The supervisor or foreman is responsible for checking to make sure that the entire Type C system is operating correctly. He or she must know the Type C system that is being used. He or she must consistently monitor the system, and be alert to the alarms. This monitoring can save lives by making sure that workers are being supplied breathable air. If you are given a Type C respirator, make sure that you and the foreman really know how the system works as instructed by the manufacturer. An untrained person must never be responsible for monitoring the system. Non - breathable air can kill workers much faster then asbestos can.

Protection factor

How much asbestos can a respirator handle? Some respirators are better than others at keeping asbestos out of your lungs. A respirator' s Protection Factor (**P**) is a measure of how well it should protect you from asbestos. Protection Factors go from 10 to 1,000+. Protection Factors are based on how respirators fit under laboratory conditions. These can be different from protection factors under actual usage due to perspiration, movement, facial features, etc. while working

A PAPR respirator has a Protection Factor of 100. (For every 100 fibers of asbestos in the air, 1 fiber leaks into the mask.)

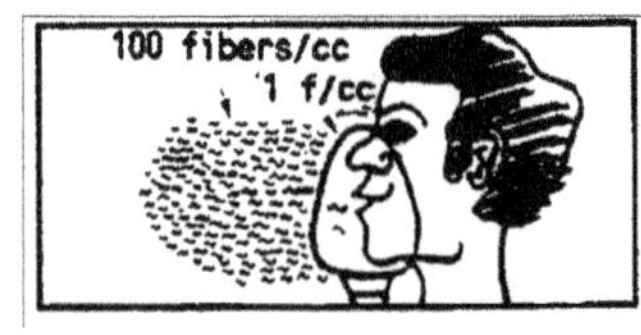

A pressure demand air supplied respirator has a Protection Factor of 1,000. (For every 1,000 fibers of asbestos, 1 fiber leaks in).

The higher the Protection Factor, the more a respirator protects you. A respirator will not protect you unless it is the right one for the job; it fits and has the right filters and parts.

A large protection factor is better than a small one.

How do you know it' s the right respirator?

When you see your air sampling results, how can you tell which respirator will protect you enough? You need to know the respirator' s limit or Maximum Use Level (MUL). This is how much asbestos the respirator can protect you from.

A half-mask, air-purifying respirator is legal up to 1 f/cc.
The Maximum Use Level is 1 f/cc.

A full-face, air-purifying respirator is legal up to 5 f/cc.
The Maximum Use Level is 5 f/cc.

A powered air - purifying respirator (PAPR) is legal up to 10 f/cc
The Maximum Use Level is 10 f/cc.

A continuous-flow Type C respirator is legal up to 10 f/cc.
The Maximum Use Level is 10 f/cc.

A pressure - demand Type C respirator is legal up to 100f/cc
The Maximum Use Level is 100f/cc.

To figure out the Maximum Use Level for a respirator, take the legal limit (the PEL=0.1) and multiply it by the Protection Factor. The Protection Factor (PF) tells you how many fibers leak in, compared to the number of fibers outside. **You need to keep the number of fibers inside below 0.1f/cc (the legal limit)**

0.1f/cc (legal limit) x Protection Factor = Maximum Use Level

0.1f/cc x PF = MUL

A Powered Air Purifying Respirator has a Protection Factor of 100.

0.1f/cc x 100 = 10f/cc

The Maximum Use Level is 10f/cc

A Pressure - Demand Air Supplied Respirator has a Protection Factor of 1,000.

0.1f/cc x 1,000 = 100f/cc

The Maximum Use Level is 100f/cc

Math review for your own information

<table>
<tr><td rowspan="2">

Number line

The numbers get bigger as you go down.

0.1 = 1/10
0.2 = 2/10 = 1/50.3 = 3/10
0.4 = 4/10
0.5 = 5/10 = 2/5
0.6 = 6/10
0.7 = 7/10
0.8 = 8/10
0.9 = 9/10
1.0 = 10/10 = 1
1.1 = 1 1/10
1.2 = 1 2/10

</td><td>

Decimals

1.0 is more than .5 ("point five")
0.5(“point five") is more than .2 ("point two")
0.2 ("point two") is more than .1 ("point one")
0.1 ("point one") is more than .01 ("point oh one")

</td></tr>
<tr><td>

Decimals and fractions

0.1 ("point one") = 1/10 ("one tenth")
0.2 ("point two") = 2/10 ("two tenths") = 1/5
0.01 ("point oh one") - 1/100 ("one one-hundredth")

</td></tr>
</table>

RESPIRATORS

Key Facts

You must wear a respirator when you work with asbestos.

You must have a doctor' s permission before you can wear a respirator on the job.

Not everyone can wear a respirator.

Respirators don' t work unless they fit properly and are the correct one for the job.

Paper dust masks are illegal for asbestos work.

Positive pressure (a motor blows air into the mask) **is better than Negative pressure** (your lungs do all the work to move the air).

A Full face mask is better than a Half face mask

Powered - Air Purifying (PAPR) (a motor does some of the work) **is better than non-powered Air - Purifying** (your lungs do all the work)

Tight - fitting (an air tight seal) **is better than Loose - fitting** (no seal)

Air supplied (brings in clean air from an outside source) **is better than Air-purifying** (filters the air in the room)

Pressure - demand (the regulator supplies more air when you breathe harder) is **better than Continuous flow** (a regulator always supplies air at the same rate)

Your employer chooses your respirators based on air sampling results and working conditions. Air supplied respirators use Grade D air.

This respirator is a powered air purifying (PAPR) Positive pressure, full - face respirator which has a protection factor of 100. It is legal up to 10 f/cc.

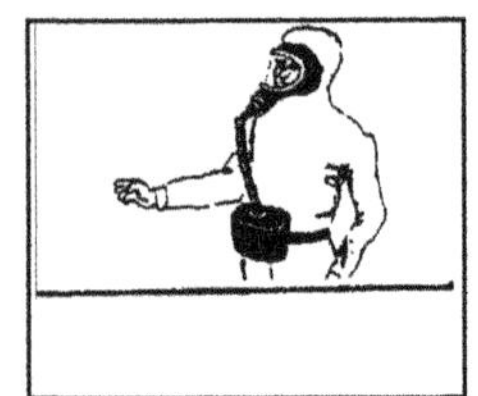

This respirator is an air-supplied (Type C) positive pressure full face pressure - demand respirator which has a protection factor of 1,000. It is legal up to 100f/cc.

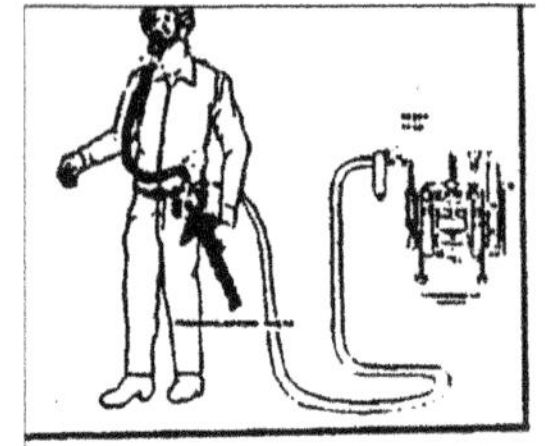

For more information

* OSHA Construction Industry Asbestos Standard, 29 CFR 1926.1101

American Lung Association, "What You Should Know About On - The - Job Respiratory Protection," ALA Item No. 0683.

* Chapter VIII. "Establishing a Type C Supplied -Air System," in "Model Curriculum for Training Asbestos Abatement Contractors and Supervisors."

*EPA/NIOSH, "A Guide to Respiratory Protection for the Asbestos Abatement Industry," Publication No. EPA-560-OPTS-86-001.3.

*NIOSH, "Respiratory Protection, A Guide for the Employee," DHHS (NIOSH) Publication No. 78-193B.

NIOSH "Guide to Industrial Respiratory Protection," DHHS (NIOSH) Publication No. 87-116.

***Your instructor may have a copy of these publications for you to look at.**

RESPIRATORS -

PART 2: CARING FOR YOUR RESPIRATOR

In this chapter you will learn:

What your employer has to do before giving you a respirator.
How to make sure your respirator fits.
How to take care of your respirator.
How to:
 clean,
 inspect,
 maintain; and
 store your respirator.

A respirator can' t protect you unless it fits

When OSHA inspects a job for health problems, more than one-third of the problems are in the company' **respirator program. The law says your employer has to have a very strong, effective respirator program.**

RESPIRATOR PROGRAM

What the employer has to do

Before your employer hands you a respirator, he or she has to do a lot of things. The employer has to find out if you can wear a respirator. Who will pick the respirators? Who will maintain them? These things have to be written down in a respirator program.

1. **Your employer must provide respirators when necessary to protect your health.**

2. **Your employer must develop and implement a written respiratory protection program that is administered by a suitably trained person.**

   Find out who the person in charge is and get a copy of the program from them.

3. **Your employer must evaluate the respiratory hazards in the workplace and identify user and workplace factors and base the respirator selection on them.**

   A gas filter won' t protect you from a dust. A dust filter won' t protect you from a gas.

A filter respirator won't protect you if there isn't enough oxygen in the air.

Your employer must determine what and how much of a contaminant you are exposed to and base the selection on that. **Under the State Employees Asbestos Program, your employer is limited to selecting either a PAPR or a Type C Pressure Demand Airline respirator for Level II building maintenance staff.**

4. **Your employer must provide medical exams to everyone who wears a respirator to determine their fitness to wear a respirator.**

No one is allowed to wear a respirator without permission from a doctor.

5. **Your employer must have you trained about respirators.**

TRAINING

Before you put on a respirator, you have to be trained. You need training on each respirator you work with. You have to learn about all the parts of your respirator. You have to learn how your respirator works. You need to know what a respirator can do for you. You need to know what a respirator can't do for you. You have to be trained in how to clean, inspect, and store your respirator. You have to have this training every year.

6. **Your employer must use approved respirators**

Respirators have to be approved by the National Institute for Occupational Safety & Health (NIOSH). All labels must comply with NIOSH and be readable.

7. **Your employer must ensure that you receive and pass a fit test.**

You must have a fit test every year!

When you first get a respirator and every year after that, the fit must be tested. You must also be fit tested when you get a new or different respirator. Remember that a respirator is only as good as its fit. There are two different kinds of **fit tests** called **qualitative or quantitative.** The tests take from ½ to 1 hour.

NOTE: If you don't work with asbestos within a 1-year period, then you do not have to be fit tested every year. You will have to be fit tested before you do the next asbestos job however, and the respirator must fit you properly. If the size you have does not fit you, then you must get a new size or brand of respirator.

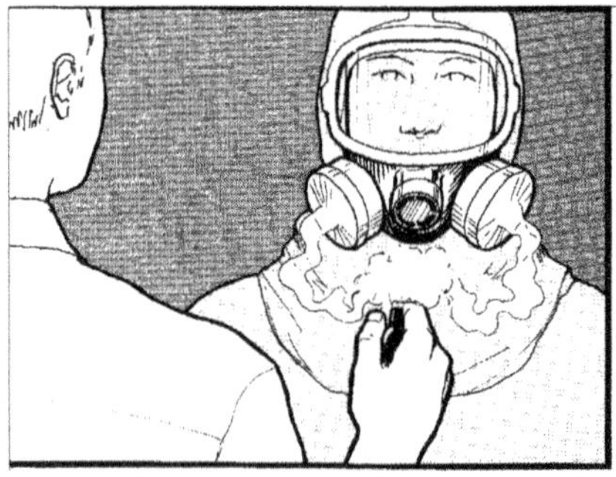

In a **qualitative fit test,** you stand in a well ventilated room and the tester pumps irritating smoke around the edges of the respirator. If the material leaks into the mask, it will cause you to cough. This means that the mask does not fit well enough to keep asbestos out of your lungs.

In a **quantitative fit test,** you will don a special respirator mask that has a probe in it. You will be tested on the same size mask that you will use for work. The probe is connected to a machine like a Port - A - Count that measures the concentration of particulate inside your mask and outside your mask. The machine will then calculate how much leakage there is.

You will have one of these fit tests during your initial training class. You must have a fit test on every respirator that you will use in your work. You must have a fit test every year and at other times between the annual fit tests whenever any of the following occur:

if you lose or gain more than 10 pounds
break your nose
lose teeth or get new dentures
have facial surgery
get glasses for the first time

8. **Your employer must establish and implement procedures for the proper use of respirators.**

9. **Your employer must provide for the cleaning, disinfecting, storage, inspection, and repair of respirators.**

   If there is anything wrong with your respirator, your employer has to fix it before you can wear it or provide you with a suitable replacement. Your employer has to check the respirators to make sure they are in good shape. Your employer has to have trained people to fix your respirator. Your employer must give you a clean, dry place to keep your respirator.

10. **Your employer must provide grade D or better breathing quality air when you use a supplied air respirator.**

11. **Your employer must evaluate the workplace to ensure that the program is working (meeting its state objectives) and that employees are using respirators properly.**

12. **Your employer must establish and retain written information regarding medical exams, fit tests, and the respirator program.**

What you have to do

After your employer gives you the respirator, you have to use it safely. Do you have the right one? Did you get a fit test on your respirator? Does the respirator work? Is it clean and sanitary?

You are the one who cares the most about whether your respirator works. If it is not in good shape, you could breathe asbestos. Learn how to properly use and take care of your respirator.

1. **Do you have the right respirator?**

Does your respirator fit you? You must get a fit test for your respirator.

Do you have an approved respirator? Look for the NIOSH seal on your respirator box and on the filters.

You need to have the right respirator for the job. Figure out which respirator you need. Is your respirator good enough? Your employer must choose the right respirator for the job.

Even if you have an approved respirator, it might not protect you enough from the amount of asbestos in the air. Respirator Protection Factors come from tests in labs.

The respirator maker tests an average size person. The tests are done in a clean, cool lab. Only a new respirator is used. But you don' t work in a lab. You may not have an average face. You sweat when you work. The respirator may slide on your face. Maybe your respirator isn' t as perfect as when it was new. There are many reasons why the respirator may not work as well for you as it did in the lab.

Respirators may not protect you as well as they are supposed to. If you can, get a **more protective respirator** than the law requires.

2. **Know how to use your respirator**

If you don' t know how to use your respirator, it will not protect you. Learn how your respirator works. If you don' t have a cleanface, the respirator will not protect you. If you don' t maintain it, the respirator will not protect you. Get to know your respirator. Get training on the respirator you use. Inspect your respirator. Are all the parts where they belong? **Always inspect your respirator before you put it on.**

3. **Inspect your respirator every time you use it**

A respirator can' t help you unless it' s in good shape. **You need to inspect your respirator before you put it on.** Make sure all the parts are there. Make sure all the parts are in good shape. Make sure all the parts are in the right place. If you find anything wrong with your respirator, do not wear it until it has been fixed.

THE PARTS OF A RESPIRATOR

All respirators have the following parts:

Inhalation Valves - This is where you breathe in. There are one or two small rubber flaps. They are about the size of a quarter.

Exhalation Valves - This is where you breathe out. It may be one or two small rubber flap(s) about the size of a quarter. It is underneath a cover. Be sure that the cover is in place or the respirator will not provide adequate protection.

Face piece - These are made of silicon, rubber, and other materials.

Straps - These hold the respirator onto your head. There are many kinds of straps. There are two straps that connect at the sides of your neck. There are two straps that connect at your temples. There is on strap that connects at your forehead.

In addition to the above parts the PAPR has:

Hose - if the motor is on your belt, this carries air up to your face.

Power Cord - if the motor is on your face, this connects the motor to the battery.

Battery - Every PAPR has a rechargeable battery to run the motor

Motor - Every PAPR has a motor either worn on a belt at your waist or on the facepiece.

Flow Tester - This device, which is separate from the respirator itself, helps to measure the airflow of the motor to the facepiece. It can help tell you if the filters need changing or the battery needs charging or it is not supplying you with the minimum required airflow needed to protect you. It can either be a wall mounted version or hand held.

Filters - These are rectangular or round in shape. They filter the asbestos out of the air.

<u>In addition to the parts common to all respirators, The Type C respirator also has:</u>

Air Regulator - This valve controls how much air comes into the mask.

Escape Air Tank - If air stops coming through the hose, you can breathe air from the air in the tank while you leave the area. (This is for escape from an IDLH atmosphere).

Face Piece Hose - This carries the air from the regulator to your face.

Airline Hose - This carries air from the tanks or compressor to the regulator.

Low Air Alarm - This device signals that air in the tanks is getting low (there is < 15 min. of air left.)

Manifold - A device that splits the regulator's single air outlet into 1- 4 outlets to supply air to 1 - 4 workers.

INSPECTING YOUR RESPIRATOR

The following are common to all respirators and should be inspected:

Inhalation Valves - Check the valves. Are they there? Are they ripped or bent? Are they dirty?

Exhalation Valves - Take off the cover (You can't do this with a Type C airline respirator). Is the valve there? Is it ripped or bent? Is it dirty? Is the cover missing?

Face piece - Is it ripped or worn? Is the face piece bent? Is it clean and sanitary?

Straps - Are they still elastic? Are they worn? Do the buckles and snaps work?

For a PAPR respirator you must check all of the above plus the following:

Hose - Is it bent or cut? Are there cracks in it?

Battery - Is it fully charged? Are back up batteries charged and ready?

Flow - Use a flow-tester each time the PAPR is used to see how much air the fan is blowing.

Filters - Do you have the right filter for the job? When you work with asbestos, you need purple (magenta) filters. Change the filters when it becomes harder to breathe. This can be caused by the filters being overloaded with asbestos or by being wet. You may have to decontaminate them before you change them.

For a Type C respirator, you need to check the parts common to all respirators as well as the following parts unique to Type C respirators:

Escape Air Tank- Is it full? Is it connected?

Face Piece Hose - Is it bent or cracked? Are there cracks in it?

Airline Hose - Is it bent or cut? Are there cracks in it?

Regulator - Can only be checked by factory-trained persons. No one else should attempt to disassemble or repair a regulator

Low Air Alarm - Must be checked by a trained person.

Air Tanks - Are they full?

Manifold - Note that all manifold connections should be capped when not in use to avoid being contaminated with grease, oil or lubricating fluids that may cause fires or explosions in contact with gases under high pressure.

Repairs

Respirator parts have to come from the same manufacturer that made the respirator. In other words, you may not use MSA brand filters on a Cesco brand respirator. You may not use 3M brand valves on an AO brand respirator. No one should fix your respirator unless he or she knows how to fix it.

4. Putting on a respirator

When you put on your full-face piece respirator, put your chin in the chin cup first. Next fit the mask to your face. Smile, frown, and move you face around. Be sure the edges of the mask fit your face. Next pull the straps over your head. Fasten the temple straps and neck straps first, then the top strap. The straps need to be tight enough to hold the respirator on your face and give you a good seal. DO NOT make them too tight. The mask will dig into your face and will be very uncomfortable to wear. Always refer to the manufacturer's instructions before putting on any respirator

5. Do fit checks every time you put on a respirator

In addition to annual fit tests that must be done every year to make sure you have the right size respirator, you also have to check the fit yourself every time you put on a respirator. The fit checks you do yourself are called a **negative pressure user seal check** and a **positive pressure user seal check. You** must do **both** of these fit checks every time you put on your PAPR respirator. (You can' t do a positive pressure fit check on a Type C respirator.)

The negative pressure user seal check. Cover the place where the hose connects to the facepiece with your hand and suck in gently. Hold for a count of ten seconds. You will feel the respirator pull against your face. You can feel the area of the seal tightening to your face. If there is a leak, air will rush in through the leak instead of pulling the facepiece against your face. You will feel air move against your cheeks. It may feel like a feather brushing across your face. The air will move toward your mouth. You may hear the airflow. If someone is watching you, they should see the respirator suck in a little at your nose if you have a good fit.

The positive pressure user seal check. Take the cover off the exhalation valve(s) on your chin or on the sides of the face piece. Cover the rubber flap(s) with your hand(s) and blow out gently. You should feel the force of your breath puff the respirator out a little bit. This is like the feeling when you first blow up a balloon. If there is a leak in the facepiece, air will rush out of the leak instead of making the mask puff out. If there is a leak, you will feel air rush out against your cheeks. You will not feel the seal tightening to your face. **Don' t blow too hard or you can blow out your inhalation valves and break a good seal.**

6. Keep your respirator clean

It is very easy to clean your respirator, and you must clean it every time you use it.

Wash the respirator in warm water (not exceeding 120 degrees) with a mild soap. You must also use an **EPA registered disinfectant that is either especially made for respirators or recommended by the manufacturer.** Wash the inside and outside of the face piece with a soft bristle brush or a clean rag. Rinse the respirator in clean water, and let it air dry. In addition to washing the face piece you need to wipe down all other parts of the respirator with a clean damp rag. Do not immerse the motor or battery of the PAPR in water.

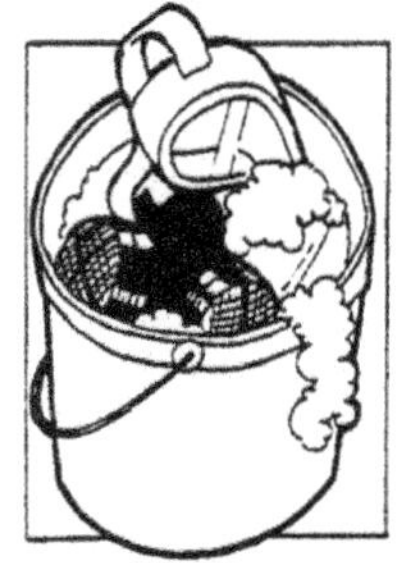

CLEANING RESPIRATOR

7. **Dry and store your respirator in a safe place**

Don' t hang your respirator by its straps to dry. This can stretch out the straps. Do not dry your respirator on a sunny window, radiator or other place that is more than 120 degrees. Too high a temperature will cause your respirator facepiece to lose its shape so that it no longer fits. Keep your respirator in a clean, dry place. Store in a clean plastic bag. It is easy to damage respirators or have them become contaminated.

CARING FOR YOUR RESPIRATOR

Key Facts

A respirator will not protect you unless it fits.

You must have a fit test before you can wear a respirator at work.

Qualitative fit testing doesn' t use machines. You use your sense of smell or taste.

Quantitative fit testing uses a machine. It measures how much air leaks around the edges of your respirator.

You must be fit tested every year.

You must inspect your respirator before you put it on.

You must do your own fit checks every time you enter an area with asbestos in it.

You must use a flow tester each time you use a PAPR to measure airflow to the facepiece.

The negative pressure user seal check: cover the inhalation valve(s) and suck in gently.

The positive pressure user seal check: cover the exhalation valve(s) and blow out gently.

You must clean your respirator with soap and water and an EPA registered disinfectant every time you use it.

Store your respirator in a clean, safe place in a clean plastic bag.

Use HEPA filters for asbestos.

Change the filters when the flow meter no longer measures in the good range. (If this doesn' t help you may need to change the battery)

Discussion questions

1. The law gives you the right to go through decontamination and wash your face if asbestos or your respirator irritates it. Why do you have this right?
2. When you first pick up your respirator, what are you going to do?
3. How often do you need a fit test?
4. Why is it important to learn how to do the positive and negative pressure fit checks?

For more information

*OSHA Respirator Standard, 29 CFR 1910.134.

American Lung Association, "What You Should Know About On-The-Job Respiratory Protection," ALA Item No. 0683.

*NIOSH, "Respiratory Protection, A Guide for the Employee," DHHS (NIOSH) Publication No. 78-193B.

*EPA/NIOSH,"A Guide to Respiratory Protection for the Asbestos Abatement Industry," Publication No. EPA-560-OPTS-86-001.

***Your instructor may have a copy of these publications for you to look at.**

Respirator exercise

This is not a test. It is an exercise. Use it to see for yourself how well you understand the material in the chapter.

1. What is the difference between a negative-pressure respirator and a positive pressure respirator?

2. Which one protects you more? Why?

3. If you are working on an abatement job and air samples show 2.5 f/cc of asbestos in the air, which respirator do you have to wear?

4. Can you request a respirator that will protect you more?

5. What is the difference between a qualitative fit test and a quantitative fit test?

6. Some people have a harder time getting a good fit on a respirator. Who are they? Why do they have a hard time?

7. Name the limits of respirators, i.e., reasons why they protect you less than they are supposed to.

8. Name two parts of a good respiratory protection program.

RESPIRATORS
Part 3: Other Safety Equipment

In this chapter you will learn:

About disposable suits.
About hard hats, boots, and other equipment.

Other Safety Equipment

A respirator is the most important piece of equipment for protecting you from asbestos. You also have to wear disposable protective clothing to protect your skin against asbestos contamination.

Asbestos workers must always wear disposable suits. The suit includes coveralls, booties, and a hood. Sometimes suits are made in one piece, sometimes in two or three. They are usually made of a papery material like Tyvek or Kleen Guard. Suits come in several sizes. Everyone in the work area must wear a suit. You may also need to wear gloves to keep asbestos off your hands.

You can make a large suit smaller by putting duct tape around the waist, wrists, and ankles. Disposable suits that are too small or just fit can rip easily. A larger suit often gives better freedom of movement. Booties are very slippery, especially on wet plastic in asbestos work areas. You may wear canvas or rubber shoes outside the booties. You may wear boots or steel-toed safety shoes. These keep you from slipping or being hurt by falling objects or electrical shocks.

You can' t take these shoes off the job unless they are cleaned. Sometimes you can clean all the asbestos off them. (Leather and fabric shoes cannot be cleaned; rubber shoes without seams can be cleaned.) If you can' t clean them, you have to throw them out or tie them up in a bag. Your employer can take them from job to job in a sealed plastic bag with a warning label on it.

You should not wear street clothes on an asbestos job. You do not want to take any asbestos home with you on your clothes. If you use any non- disposable equipment (such as work boots or a hard hat) on an asbestos job, you must clean it. Do not take it off the job unless it is clean. Your employer can take it from job to job in a sealed, labeled, plastic bag.

Disposable suits are the only ones that you can use in the State of Maryland. If you work in cold weather, you will probably wear long underwear. It should not leave the job.

If you take asbestos home on your skin or street clothes, fibers can come off in your home. Your family could get Asbestosis, Mesothelioma, or other asbestos diseases if they breathe or swallow asbestos. It is very important to wear a suit and not take your work clothes home.

Asbestos work has many of the same dangers as ordinary demolition work. You need to wear latex, cotton, or leather gloves if you work with sharp metal lath or around hot pipes or if you are working with thermal system insulation or surfacing materials in amounts greater than 10 SQ. FT. or 25 LIN. FT. You need to wear steel - toed safety boots and hard hats if building materials might fall.

WEAR A SUIT AND A RESPIRATOR

You should have some training about how to use safety equipment in accordance with OSHA regulations. For example, hard hats are made to protect you if something falls straight down on your head. But they will not protect you if something hits you from the side. Your employer should train you about hard hats. OSHA has rules about protective equipment like hard hats, goggles, and boots. Many of the rules for respirators also apply to other equipment. For example, goggles will not protect you unless they are in good shape. They have to be cleaned, stored, maintained, and inspected for defects.

OTHER PROTECTIVE EQUIPMENT

Key Facts

You must wear disposable protective clothing on an asbestos job.

Asbestos work is just as dangerous as other demolition work.

You may need to wear a hard hat, goggles, or steel- toed boots outside your disposable suit.

For more information

*OSHA Personal Protective Equipment Standards, 1910.132, 1910.133, 1910.135, 1910.136.

*OSHA, "Personal Protective Equipment," Publication No. OSHA 3077.

***Your instructor may have copies of these publications for you to look at.**

CHAPTER 5

CONTROL METHODS

In this chapter you will learn:

How asbestos can be controlled.
About the kind of asbestos work you may do.

Control Methods

When asbestos materials are found in a building, the owner of the building must make a decision about what to do with them. The danger from asbestos materials depends on how likely they are to release fibers into the air. Products, which are in good shape and are unlikely to be damaged by accident, are not a problem. These products can stay in the building and might not be removed until the building is renovated or demolished.

Products, which are in bad shape, need to have something done to them to prevent fibers from getting into the building air. There are a number of different ways to do this. These are called **control methods**. The **control methods**, which may be used, are:

1. **Operations & Maintenance**
2. **Repair**
3. **Encapsulation**
4. **Enclosure**
5. **Removal**
6. **Restriction**

These Control Methods are sometimes used together on one project. For example, a job may involve the removal of 100 feet of pipe covering and repair of an additional 1000 feet. Or encapsulation of most of the ceiling material in a building, but removal of the material which is in areas where the hallway is low.

Usually, asbestos workers and supervisors will not decide which method to use. That decision is made by the building owner and a Project Designer accredited under the Model Accreditation Program. The selected method(s) are then included in the job specifications (specs) for the project.

1. Operation and Maintenance

An Operations and Maintenance program is a control method used for managing asbestos while it remains in a building. It must be developed by an asbestos Management Planner accredited under the Model Accreditation Program. An Operations and Maintenance program should be set up in any building, which has asbestos in it. The program has a number of different parts. They are listed below:

1. A list or inventory of all asbestos materials in the building is made. The inventory includes what kinds of materials, where they are located, how much there is, and what kind of shape they' re in.

2. Materials in the building must be labeled with stickers to alert workers that they contain asbestos. Signs may need to be posted in areas that contain asbestos.

3. The materials are checked at least every six months to see if they are still in good shape.

4. Training is done for maintenance employees so that they can handle small amounts of asbestos that might be disturbed during their work.

5. Work procedures are developed for maintenance work. For example, how to safely remove and dispose of a small amount of pipe insulation so that a leaking pipe valve could be repaired.

6. Proper equipment is provided to maintenance workers so that they can do the work safely.

7. Procedures are developed for dealing with accidental damage to asbestos materials such as fiber release episodes.

The point of the Operations and Maintenance program is to prevent the asbestos materials from releasing fibers into the building. This protects maintenance and service workers, outside contractors (plumbers, electricians, etc.) and other people in the building. All of the parts of the program are important. If some parts are done but others are not, the program won' t be effective. A good Operations and Maintenance program also requires that the building owner have a knowledgeable person on staff who has the authority deal with asbestos related issues. The building engineer or someone else should be trained to know about asbestos hazards and how to run the owner' s program.

2. Repair

Repair is a control method, which can be used if there are small amounts of damage to asbestos materials. For example, asbestos pipe insulation might have a canvas covering which is torn and the tear exposes the asbestos fibers that can be released into the air. Wrapping new canvas around the tear and repainting it, is considered a repaired.

3. Encapsulation

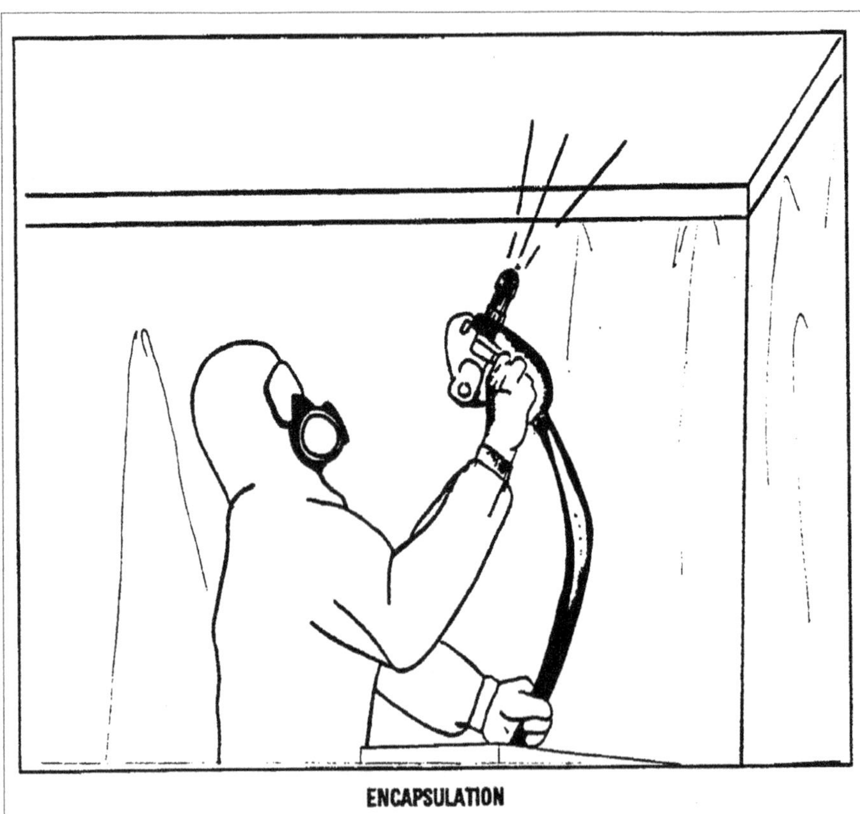

ENCAPSULATION

Encapsulation is the spraying or brushing on of a paint-like coating over the asbestos-containing material. The coating is put on with either a **low-pressure sprayer** or a brush. When material is encapsulated, the coating prevents release of asbestos fibers into the air. The coating can also prevent some damage to the material from contact.

When you work on an encapsulation job, you can still be exposed to asbestos fibers. In fact, when the encapsulant hits the material a small amount of dust is sometimes released into the air. The material cannot be wetted first, because the encapsulant will not stick. Because of this, an encapsulation job is set up just like a removal job. Workers will also wear respirators and disposable protective clothing while doing encapsulation.

Two kinds of encapsulants are used. One kind is called a **bridging encapsulant.** This kind covers the material with a "tough skin" on the outside. The other kind is called a **penetrating encapsulant**. This kind soaks into the material and binds the material together. The material then becomes hard like a plaster cast.

When doing encapsulation, workers usually apply two coats over the material depending on the manufacturer' s instructions. This is done to make sure that the asbestos is completely covered. The encapsulant takes some time to dry. Materials contaminated with dust during the job are disposed of as asbestos waste. This includes plastic barriers, suits, and other items.

4. Enclosure

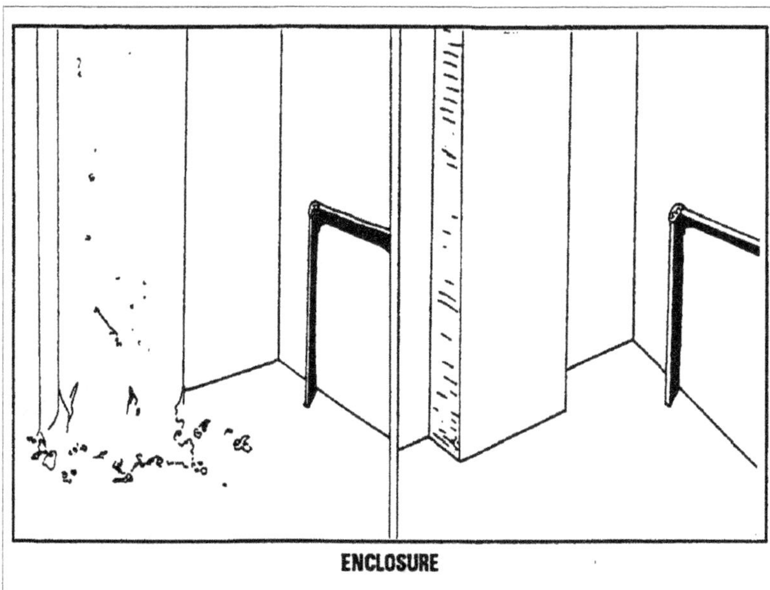

ENCLOSURE

Enclosure means building an airtight barrier around asbestos containing materials. The enclosure is built with non-asbestos building materials. Examples are sheet rock, wood, and spline joints, caulked sheet metal and other materials. **If the barrier is not airtight, it is not considered an enclosure.** For example, putting in a drop ceiling to control asbestos fireproofing material is not an enclosure.

An enclosure job also requires that containment be built. Building the enclosure often requires disturbing the material. Workers will also have to wear respirators and protective clothing. If drills or nail guns are used to attach the enclosure, asbestos dust can be released. Another type of enclosure is sometimes referred to as **encasement**. Encasement means spraying a closed cell foam directly on an asbestos material or onto a lattice hung below the material. Another example would be to pour concrete onto a dirt floor in a crawl space.

During an enclosure job, disturb the material as little as possible. It is best to use power tools such as drills only if they are attached to a HEPA vacuum. Items from the work area (like plastic sheeting and suits) that get dust on them have to be disposed of as asbestos waste. Other things like power tools must be cleaned before they leave the containment.

5. Removal

Removal is the method used most to control fiber release from asbestos materials in buildings. Removal means taking the asbestos off of whatever it is on. Except in rare circumstances, asbestos is always wetted before it is removed. It is then bagged and sealed and taken to a landfill that accepts asbestos and is licensed to do so. A removal job must not only remove the material that can be easily seen but also the fibers you cannot see. Workers will also be doing lots of cleaning. This is because when asbestos is scraped, pulled, or ripped off surfaces or mechanical systems, many fibers are released. These must be cleaned up as part of the removal job.

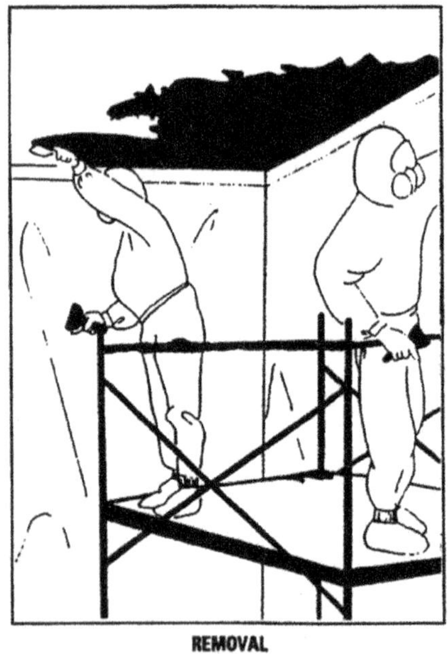
REMOVAL

On a removal job you can be exposed to a lot of asbestos fibers. This is why strong rules have been made for these jobs. If removal jobs are not done right, **workers can be exposed to asbestos. In addition, a poor removal job can leave more asbestos fibers in the building air than there were before.**

These two reasons are why it is so important to use the methods and follow the rules, which we will talk about in the rest of the manual.

6. Restriction

Restriction is a control method, which is often used for areas, which do not require frequent access or in cases where funding is limited. Restriction means that the area can only be accessed by trained and medically monitored Level II personnel. These Level II employees must be wearing a respirator and a disposable suit when working in restricted areas. Areas are restricted which have asbestos that is damaged and cannot be abated right away.

CONTROL METHODS

KEY FACTS

Asbestos in buildings can be controlled in a number of different ways.

The different ways are:

1. Encapsulation
2. Enclosure
3. Removal
4. Repair
5. Operations and Maintenance Program
6. Restriction

An **Operations and Maintenance Program** (O&M) is a written program. It is needed when asbestos will remain in a building. The written O&M program includes:

1. Where asbestos is found.
2. Signs & labeling of asbestos containing materials.
3. Worker training requirements.
4. Ways to work with asbestos safely. This includes equipment, worker protection, and medical exams.
5. Permits, which are required before beginning, work.
6. How to check the condition of asbestos materials and record any changes.
7. Recordkeeping

Repair means fixing small areas of damaged asbestos material

Encapsulation means spraying or brushing a paint like coating over the asbestos material. This binds the material together.

Enclosure means building an airtight barrier around the asbestos material.

Removal means taking off the asbestos material from whatever it is on, cleaning the material up, and properly disposing of it.

Restriction means access to the area is limited to properly trained and equipped Level II personnel.

Discussion Questions

1. What kind of material do you think would not be good to encapsulate?
2. Can you see a situation in which more than one control method might be used in an area?

For more information

*Guidance for Controlling Asbestos Containing Materials in Buildings (The Purple Book), U.S. Environmental Protection Agency, June 1985.

*Managing Asbestos in Place, A Building Owner' s Guide to Operations and Maintenance Programs for Asbestos Containing Materials (The Green Book), U.S. Environmental Protection Agency, July 1990.

***Your instructor may have a copy of these materials for you to look at.**

SETUP

In this chapter you will learn:

How to keep asbestos out of the air.
About wearing a respirator and disposable suit.
What an asbestos job looks like.
How to clean the work room.
How to set up the work room.

KEEP ASBESTOS OUT OF THE AIR

Six basic rules for working with asbestos:

1. *keep the asbestos wet*
2. *contain the work area*
3. *filter the air*
4. *use negative air pressure*
5. *practice good housekeeping*
6. *dispose of waste properly*

No matter how good your respirator is, some asbestos will leak in. So one of the best ways to keep asbestos out of your lungs is to **keep it out of the air.** There are many ways to keep asbestos out of the air. These are called **work practice controls** and **engineering controls.**

There are **six basic rules for working with asbestos.** Follow these rules when you take asbestos out of a whole room or off a single pipe. Follow these rules when you set up a job. Follow these rules when you take down the asbestos and properly dispose of it. Follow these rules when you clean up the work area.

1. Keep the asbestos wet

When you work on asbestos, you must keep it wet. Dry, fluffy asbestos can send up a cloud of fibers you can' t even see. The fibers are so light they can float in the air for days.

When the asbestos is wet, the fibers stick together. When you spray water into the air or onto the asbestos, fibers are trapped by drops of water. The fibers are pulled down to the ground, out of the air. To make the water soak into the asbestos faster, always add a chemical called **surfactant** that is a soap-like solution. Surfactant makes the water wetter. Water with **surfactant** in it is called **amended water.**

Get the asbestos wet before you cut it or even touch it. Do this when you are working on a large job or a small one. Do this when you are setting up, removing asbestos, disposing of it, or cleaning up.

USE WATER TO CLEAN UP

2. Contain the work area

Cover the surfaces that will not be abated (generally the walls and floor of the work room), with plastic. Use polyethylene sheet plastic, which must be 6 mil thick. On the job it is usually called **poly** (pronounced polly).

Putting up poly does four things:

1. It protects the walls and floor from water and asbestos.
2. It keeps asbestos from spreading outside the work area.
3. It keeps everyone but workers away from the asbestos.
4. It makes clean up easier.

The plastic must be airtight. Put up plastic on large jobs and small jobs. When working on a whole room, use a full containment. When working on a small section of pipe, use a mini enclosure or a glove bag. All of these except the glovebag will consist of two layers of 6-mil poly.

3. Filter the air

Any air that has asbestos in it must be filtered before it is released from the work area. You must use a filter that is so fine it can remove the asbestos in the air. It is called a High Efficiency Particulate Air filter (HEPA-filter). A HEPA filter takes out 99.97% of all particles 0.3 microns or larger. (A micron is very small. More than 25,000 fit in one inch).

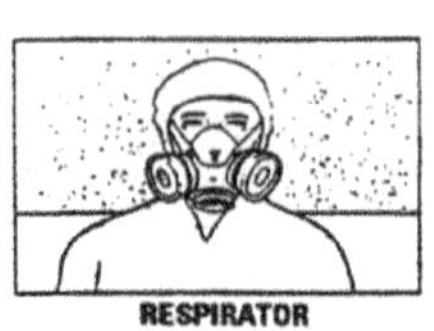

RESPIRATOR

HEPA VACUUM

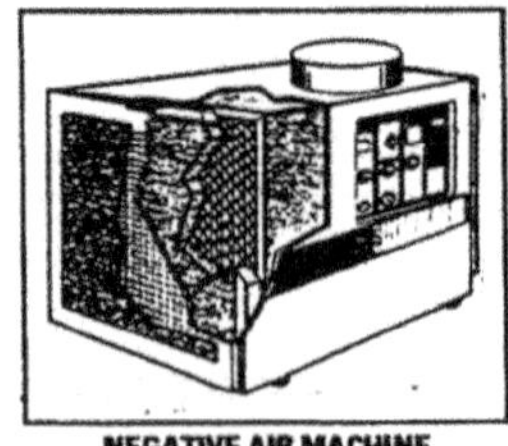

NEGATIVE AIR MACHINE

Respirators, vacuum cleaners, and negative air machines (see above); all must have HEPA filters in them so that the air will be as free as possible from asbestos fibers.

Never use an ordinary shop vacuum for asbestos work. The vacuum has a paper or other filter that will not trap asbestos. You will blow asbestos into the air. You must use an industrial vacuum with HEPA filters (a HEPA vac) when you work with asbestos.

4. Use negative air pressure

Put a heavy-duty fan with HEPA filters at one end of the work area. This is called a negative air machine. The fan pulls dirty air into the negative air machine. The HEPA filters remove the asbestos. All the air that leaves the room is "clean".

The negative air machine also pulls clean air in from across the work area through the flaps at the entrance to the work area from the decon area. It makes the work area a little cooler.

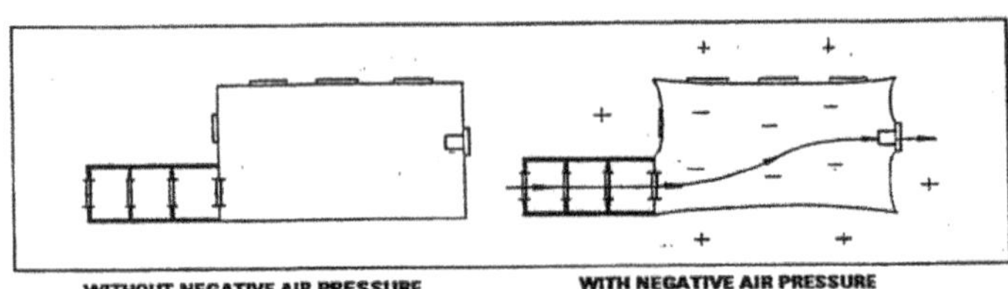

WITHOUT NEGATIVE AIR PRESSURE WITH NEGATIVE AIR PRESSURE

This system creates a negative pressure in the work area relative to adjacent areas. Thus, if there is a small leak in the containment, clean air will rush in instead of contaminated air leaking out of the work area. If the leak in the containment is substantial however, negative pressure will be lost and the asbestos contamination will spread to surrounding areas. Use negative pressure on both large and small jobs. On a large job use a negative air machine to provide negative pressure. On a small job use a HEPA filtered vacuum to provide negative air pressure.

5. Practice good housekeeping

To reduce fiber release, good housekeeping is a must. This means that you do not let asbestos pile up on the floor where it can dry out and be reintroduced into the air. Bag the asbestos as you are removing it, **while it is still wet**. In addition, you must never drop or throw asbestos.

6. Properly dispose of waste

All asbestos containing waste must be disposed of in 6mil specially labeled bags or fiber drums. It must be sent to an EPA approved landfill. It must be transported in an enclosed truck. You cannot take the waste just anywhere.

After you follow these six basic rules, there may still be some asbestos in the air. You must wear a respirator and you must wear a disposable suit every time you work with asbestos.

KEEPING ASBESTOS OUT OF THE AIR

Key Facts

One of the best ways to keep asbestos out of your lungs is to keep it out of the air.

Six basic rules for keeping asbestos out of the air:

1. Keep the asbestos wet.
   Wet down the asbestos material before you handle it.
   To make the water soak into the asbestos faster, add a chemical called surfactant.
   Water with surfactant in it is called amended water.

2. Contain the work area with plastic (poly).
   The plastic can be as large as a work area or as small as a glove bag.

3. Filter the air with High Efficiency Particulate Air filters (HEPA filters).
   Use a respirator with HEPA filters.
   Use a HEPA vacuum.
   Use a negative air machine to clean the air that leaves the work area.

4. Use negative air pressure.
   Use a negative air machine to clean the air.

4. Practice Good Housekeeping – bag waste while wet, don't drop or throw it

5. Properly Dispose of all waste – must go to approved landfill

After you do all these things, there will still be asbestos in the air.

You must wear a respirator and a disposable suit every time you work with asbestos.

Discussion Questions

1. Why not try to spread asbestos fibers around and lower the concentration in the air?

2. Why won' t fibers leak out if there is a negative air machine set up?

For more information

*OSHA Asbestos Standard, 29 CFR 1926.1101

{add NESHAP adequately wet guide}

Your instructor may have a copy of this publication for you to look at.

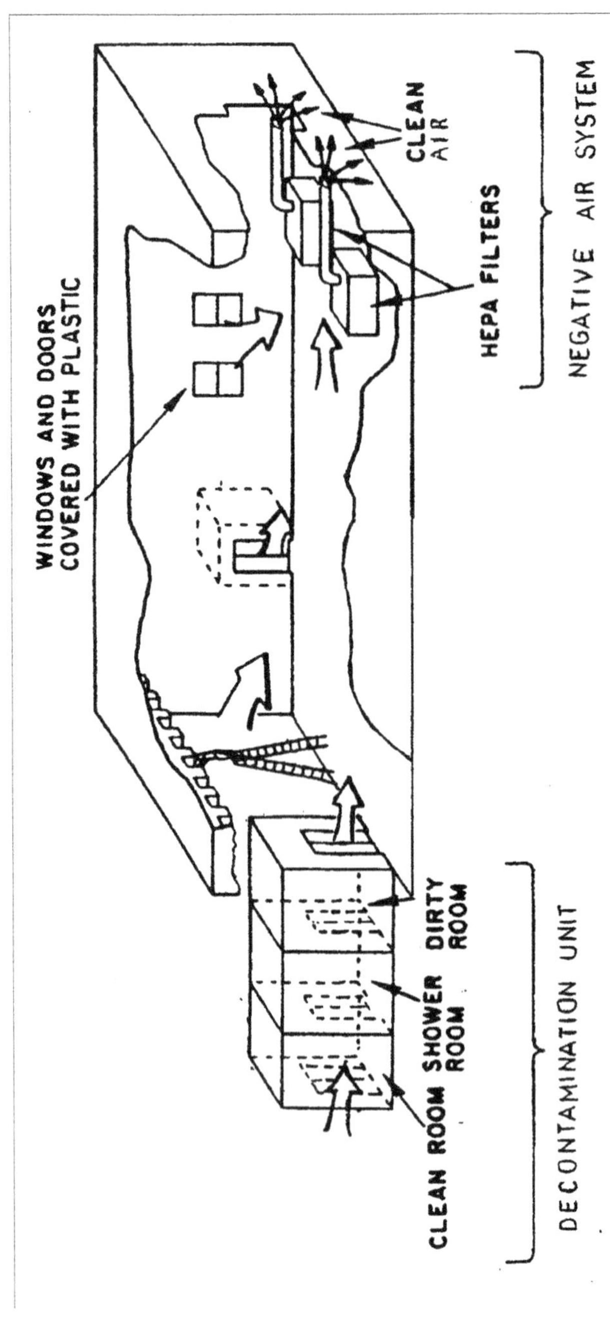
WINDOWS AND DOORS COVERED WITH PLASTIC
CLEAN AIR
HEPA FILTERS
NEGATIVE AIR SYSTEM
CLEAN ROOM
SHOWER ROOM
DIRTY ROOM
DECONTAMINATION UNIT
WORK ROOM

SET UP - OVERVIEW

By now, you know that protecting your lungs with respirators and wearing disposable suits is very important. You also know about some ways to keep asbestos out of the air. One way to do this is to cover the walls and floor with 2 layers of 6-mil sheet plastic (Poly.) This keeps the asbestos in the work area. It keeps it out of the rest of the building.

Now you will apply the rules you have learned to a large asbestos removal job. **Keep the asbestos wet, contain the work area, filter the air, use negative air pressure, practice good housekeeping and properly dispose of all asbestos containing waste.**

When you take asbestos off a whole ceiling, build a **full containment.** Do this when you take asbestos off a whole run of pipes or air ducts or a whole wall or remove floor tiles. Cover the walls and floor with **2 sheets of 6 mil plastic (poly).** Seal off all the exits except one. Build a **decontamination unit** or **decon** there. If you are removing more than 10 sq. ft. or 25 lin. ft. of asbestos you will need a decontamination unit that has a clean room, a shower room, and an equipment room all separated from each other, the outside, and the work room by double flap "doorways" made of 6-mil thick poly. If you are removing less than these amounts then an equipment room or area will be all that is required. Set up a **negative air machine** at the other end of the room.

Most of this manual is based on what OSHA regulations say you have to do as well as the State Employees Asbestos Program requirements.

SETUP

Setup is at least 40% of an asbestos job.

Experienced asbestos companies know that **a good setup is at least 40% of an asbestos job.** Before you even touch the asbestos, you have to **cover the room with 6 mil sheet plastic (poly). You have to turn off both the existing ventilation and electrical systems in the work area. You have to clean and protect the room. You have to bring in extension cords for your lights and negative air machines.** Good setup makes the rest of your job much easier. It also prevents many safety problems.

For jobs over 3 sq. Ft. or 3 lin. Ft., an **accredited Project Designer** must write up how the job will be done. This should tell you how to setup the work room. An **accredited Supervisor** must supervise setup. The supervisor is called the **"competent person".**

Before you do any work, find out if you need to put on a suit and respirator. **Remember:** If there is any possibility of asbestos being disturbed during set-up, you must wear a suit and respirator. Set up the work room in this order:

1. Notify affected parties and put up warning signs
2. Shut off the ventilation system, lock out the controls, and cover and seal vents.
3. Shut off the electrical system and lock out the controls.
4. Bring in extension cords.
5. Bring scaffolds and tools into the room.
6. Build the decontamination (decon).
7. Hook up and start the negative air machine.
8. Clean everything in the room.
9. Throw out what you can' t clean.
10. Take out anything you can move.
11. Wrap anything you can' t move in poly.
12. Cover all openings **(Critical Barriers)** in the room with 2 layers of 6 mil. plastic (poly).
13. Put two layers of poly on the floor.
14. Put two layers of poly on the walls.

1. Notify affected parties and put up warning signs

Notify building occupants and employees of intentions involving asbestos. Put up a barrier outside the work area. This will keep non-workers out. Hang asbestos warning signs on the barrier. The signs must look exactly like this one. The signs should be at eye level. They should be in a language that building users can read.

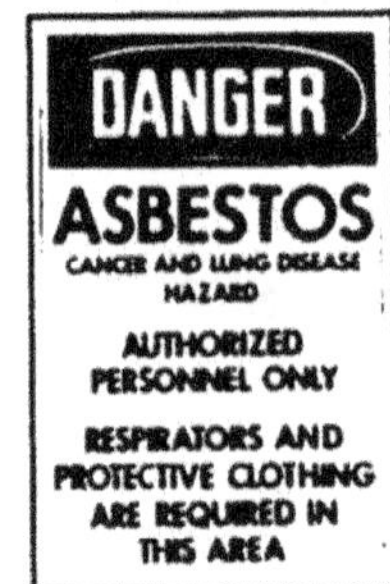

OSHA SIGN

2. Shut off the ventilation system

The ventilation system carries air through the building. **It can carry asbestos through the building**. Asbestos goes where air goes. The ventilation system for the work area must be shut off. Shut off the system at the electrical box. Lock the box and label it with a tag. Cover and seal vent openings with 6-mil thick plastic. The ventilation system is often called the **HVAC system.** HVAC stands for Heating, Ventilation, and Air Conditioning.

3. Shut off the electrical system

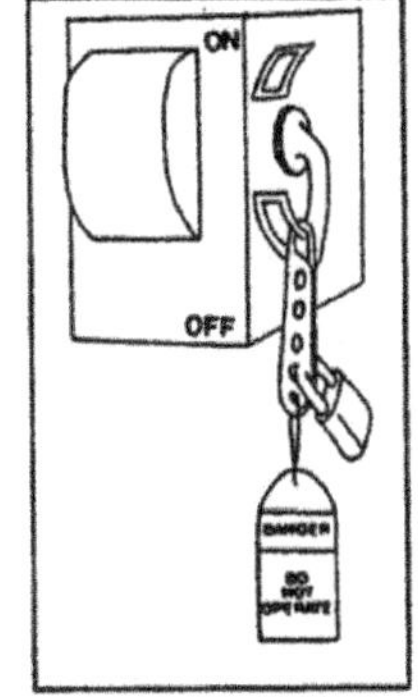

LOCK ELECTRICAL BOXES

Asbestos jobs are wet. Electrical shocks are one of the worst dangers on an asbestos job. Water can leak into an electrical outlet and kill you. The electrical system must be shut off. Shut off the system at the electrical box. Lock the box and label it with a tag. **Turning off wall switches is not enough. Someone who doesn' t know about asbestos work could electrocute you by mistake by throwing a switch that is not locked and tagged out.** Machines and other mechanical systems also have to be shut off. A machine with moving parts could hurt someone. It has to be turned off and locked so that people can work safely around it.

Steam pipes and other energized sources have to be shut off too. Let the pipes cool for at least 12 hours before working on them.

4. Bring in extension cords

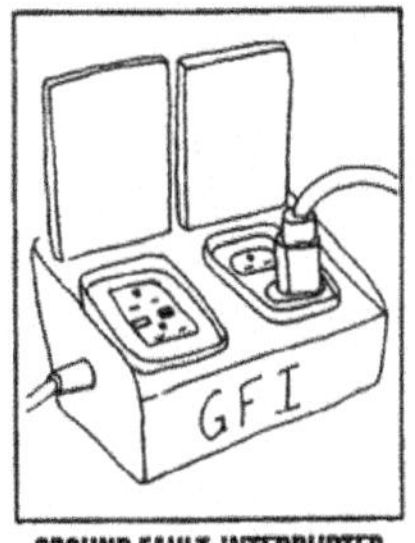

GROUND FAULT INTERRUPTER

Negative air machines, safety lights, HEPA vacuums, and tools all need power. Bring in extension cords for all the equipment. Extension cords are sometimes called **temporary wiring. Tape the cords onto the walls so that workers won' t trip on them. Do not hang cords with metal wire.** This could cause a shock. Cords must be hooked up to sensitive circuit breakers. These are called **Ground Fault Circuit Interrupters (GFCI' s).**

5. Bring scaffolds and tools into the room

Scaffolds may be too big to bring through the decontamination unit (decon). Bring the scaffolds in before the decon is assembled. Put tape over any open the ends of the scaffolds so that asbestos won' t fall in. Bring in any large equipment. Be sure that all the tools you need are in the work area before removal begins.

6. Build the decontamination unit (decon)

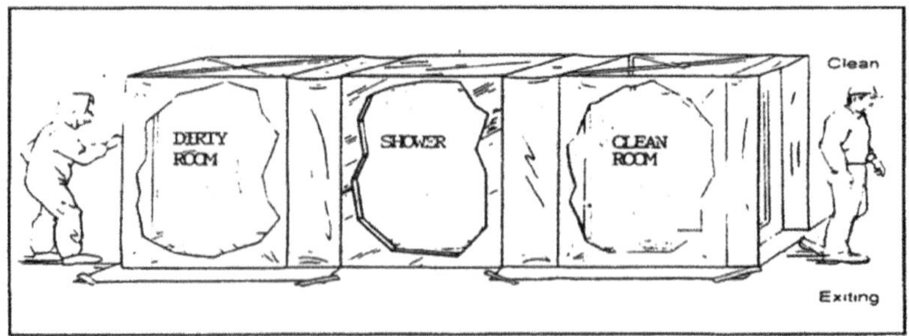

DECONTAMINATION UNIT (DECON)

You go into and leave the work room through a special area. It is called the decontamination unit (decon). The decon has a shower. Every time you leave the work room, you must take a shower or wash off. Don' t take asbestos out ofhe work room on your body with you. The decon has three rooms. They have to be in this order (starting from the work room):

Work area - Dirty room - Shower - Clean room

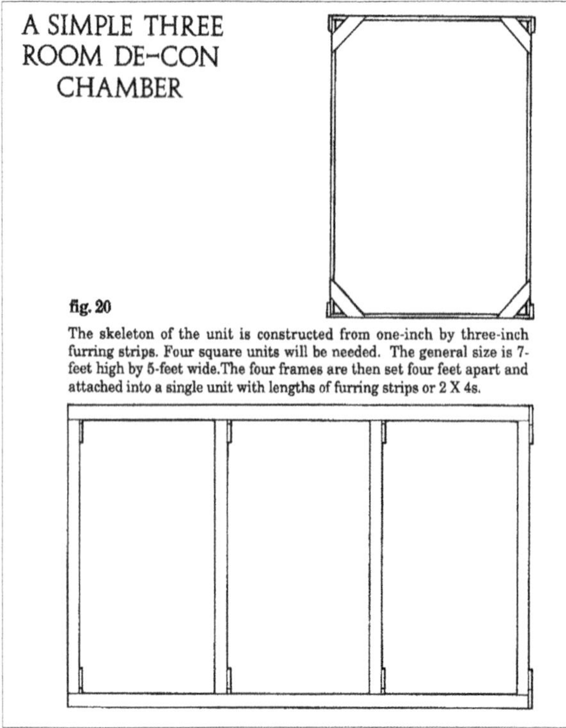

fig. 20

The skeleton of the unit is constructed from one-inch by three-inch furring strips. Four square units will be needed. The general size is 7-feet high by 5-feet wide.The four frames are then set four feet apart and attached into a single unit with lengths of furring strips or 2 X 4s.

The decon is lined with two layers of 6-mil thick poly and duct tape. The rooms have plastic flaps between them. The flaps keep air from moving out, but let air come in. Seal the decon air- tight to the work area. Make sure the base plastic (poly) extends one foot up the side framing. This ensures that any asbestos laden water will not leak out.

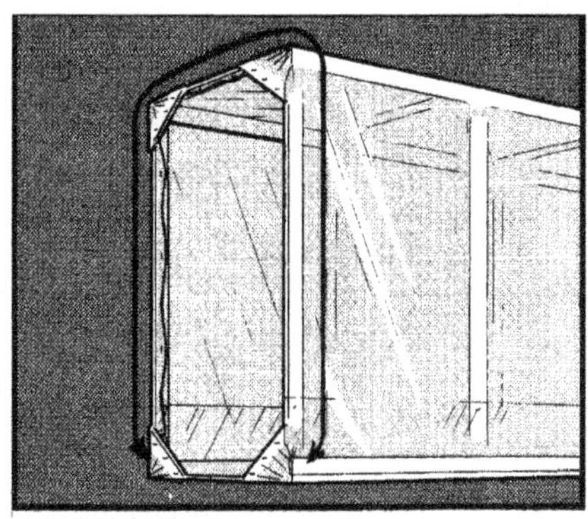

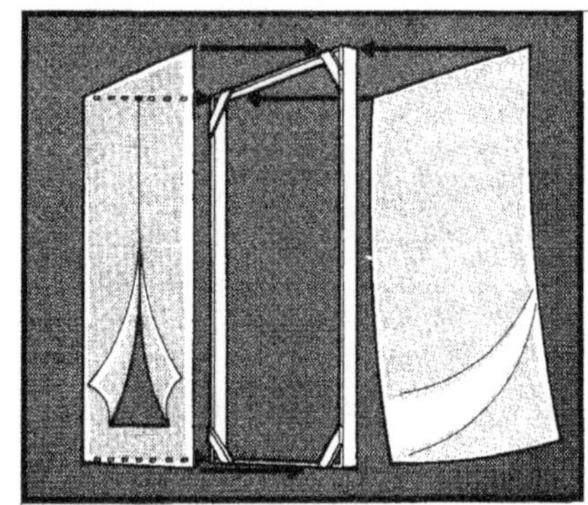

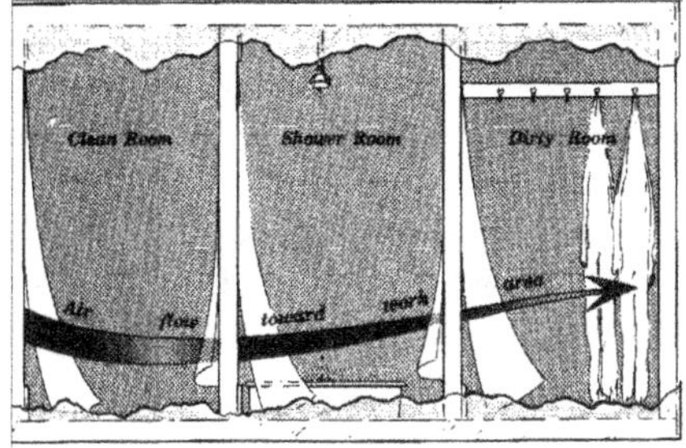

Some decons have extra empty rooms (airlocks) between the three main chambers. These keep air from moving out through the decon. Some new decons have solid doors with gaskets (rubber strips around the edge). Air comes in through HEPA filters or flaps built into the walls of the decon or work room.

Some contractors build their own decons. They use wood, pipes, poly, spray glue, and tape. Some contractors use hard plastic decons. Others use decon trailers that go outside the building. Sometimes a separate decon is built for waste bags and tools. This is called a **waste load out.**

7. Hook up and start the negative air machine

The filtered air from the negative air machine goes out a window to the outside. The seal at the window has to be airtight. Cut holes in a piece of plywood and tape the hose in. If you are working in a large room, there will be more than one machine.

NEGATIVE AIR MACHINE

Put the negative air machine as far away as possible from the decon. Air should be pulled away from workers across the longest possible distance from the decon. You may have to use hoses if the only window in the room is right next to the decon. If there is more than one machine, they should all be on the side of the room farthest from the decon. When the negative air machine is on, air comes into the room through the decon. The negative air machine should be on 24 hours a day until the project passes final clearance air monitoring. **Air should only leak in, not out.** Sometimes extra holes are cut in the poly so that enough air will come in. This is called **makeup air**. These holes <u>must</u> be covered on the inside with plastic flaps or HEPA filters in case the negative air machine shuts down.

8. Clean everything in the room

You might do a great job of scraping the asbestos off a ceiling. But what about the asbestos dust that was on the furnishings and surfaces before you started the job? Asbestos dust must be cleaned up. If you don' t clean before you take the asbestos off, the room will still be dirty at the end of the job. **Clean everything in the room before you put up the poly (plastic).** In this situation be sure to wear your respirator and disposable protective clothing. Use damp rags and HEPA vacuums. When you clean, you may get asbestos in the air. Even if you can' t see it, the asbestos may be there.**As soon as you start to handle asbestos, put on a respirator and disposable suit. Your employer should test the air.** You must have permission from a doctor before you may wear a respirator. You must pass a fit test before you may wear a respirator.

Clean everything in the room:

- walls
- electrical outlets
- floors
- paintings
- window sills
- posters
- furniture
- books
- air vents
- office equipment
- office supplies
- machines
- circuit breakers
- fuse boxes
- lights
- non-moveable objects

Clean the surface air vents with damp rags and HEPA vacuums. Wet the filters and dispose of them with the asbestos. After deactivating the power, clean electrical outlets with HEPA vacuums. If needed, clean **de-energized** circuit breakers and fuse boxes with HEPA Vacuums. Clean the lights inside and out with HEPA vacuums.

Clean carefully, starting at the top of the walls and working down. Fold the rags periodically to expose a new clean portion of the rag, **otherwise you will spread asbestos onto places you' ve already cleaned.**The rags have to be thrown out as asbestos-containing waste.

9. Dispose of what you can' t clean

Contaminated rugs and fabric on furniture must be disposed of. Wrap the rug in two layers of 6 mil poly (plastic). Seal it up with duct tape and put a label on it. The label must contain the same information as the OSHA label. Send the rug to an asbestos landfill.

RUG WRAPPED UP

10. Take out anything you can move

Move anything you can out of the room:

- chairs
- office supplies
- books
- desks
- machines
- air grates
- computers
- paintings
- lights
- cabinets
- posters
- bookshelves

There is no excuse for piling furniture in a corner of the room. Even if you cover it with poly, it will get asbestos or water on it. Lights should always be taken out unless they can' t be moved.

11. Wrap anything in poly you can' t move

Those objects that you can' t move must be sealed. Wrap them in two layers of 6-mil thick poly and duct tape. Put tape on all of the seams. Tape the poly to the floor. The poly has to be totally sealed, not just draped over the machine.

Sinks and water fountains also have to be sealed in two layers of 6 mil poly. Shut them off at the valve. Label them with DO NOT DRINK signs. **You may not use the sinks or electrical boxes in the room during the job.**

Seal up electrical boxes, blackboards, thermostats, alarms, and anything else that must stay in the room. In places like boiler rooms you may have to seal off a working machine. This is hard, since poly will melt and can burn at 150 degrees. Machines give off heat and may also need air to work. You may need to build an enclosure around the machine. You have to keep asbestos out of the machine without staring a fire. **If machines cannot be shut off or safely enclosed, State employees cannot do that asbestos job. It must be contracted out.**

12. Cover all windows and openings to the room

In the work area, replacement air should only come through the decontamination unit (decon)

Air should only go out through the negative air machine. Seal up any other places where air can go into or out of the room. **Cover windows and doors with two layers of 6-mil thick poly and duct tape.** Leave part of one window uncovered for the negative air machine.

COVER AIR VENTS WITH POLY

Cover all these places:

- windows
- air vents
- electrical outlets
- doors
- light wells (where lights were taken out)
- pipe chases (where pipes go through a wall)

Cover air vents with two layers of poly. Seal them with duct tape. Seal the poly so that no water and no air can get in or out. Cover light wells with two layers of poly and duct tape. If you can' take the lights out, seal them up with poly and tape. The poly over windows and other openings that communicate with other areas is called a **"critical barrier".**

13. Put poly on the floor

The first layer of poly goes on the floor. **Cut the poly big enough so that it goes up the walls at least one foot.** Tape all the way around the edges of the poly.

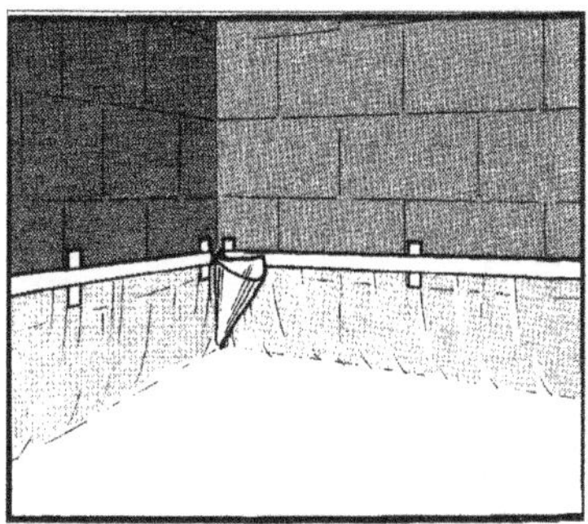

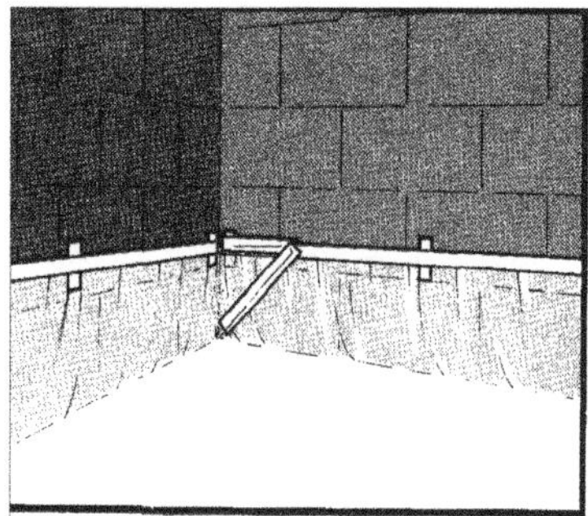

The idea is to build a watertight plastic basin inside the room. The poly on the floor should catch all of the asbestos and water. Air and water should not leak out of this basin. Try to cover the whole floor with one piece of poly. If this is not possible**, overlap the pieces of plastic 12 inches**. Any seams in the poly, have to be sealed. Use duct tape. It is a good idea to put a line of blue carpenter' s chalk under the seams. If water and asbestos leak through, they will make the chalk dark. Then you can clean them up before they damage the floor. There may be seams in both layers of poly. Put the seams from the top layer of poly at least 6 feet apart from the seams on the bottom layer. Then a leak in the top layer won' t leak through the bottom layer. **The Poly on the floor should extend up the wall at least 12 inches.**

14. Put poly on the walls

Cut the poly big enough so that it comes down at least one foot onto the floor. There should be at least a one-foot overlap between the poly on the floor and on the walls. Tape the poly on the top of the walls.

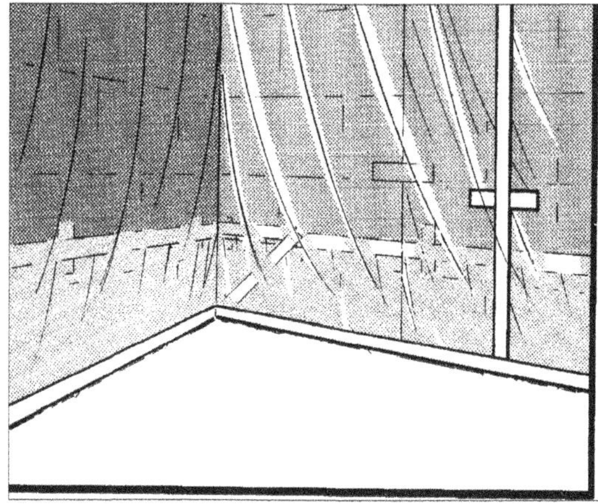

Don' t tape it one or two feet down from the ceiling Remember that the poly has to make an airtight and watertight bubble inside the room. It protects the walls from asbestos and water. If the top of the wall is not covered, it may get asbestos on it. It will probably be damaged. Tape all the way around the edges of the poly at the bottom. Poly is heavy, and duct tape can come loose when it' s wet. Duct tape may not be strong enough to hold the poly on the walls. You may have to nail furring strips (small pieces of wood) to the walls. Staple the poly to the furring strips. Put duct tape over all the staples and the edge of the poly.

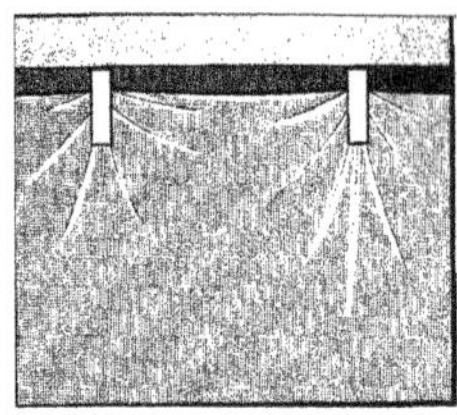
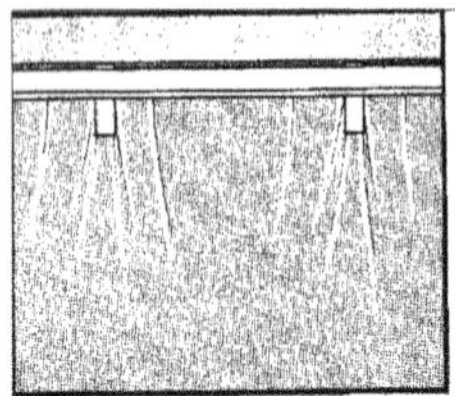
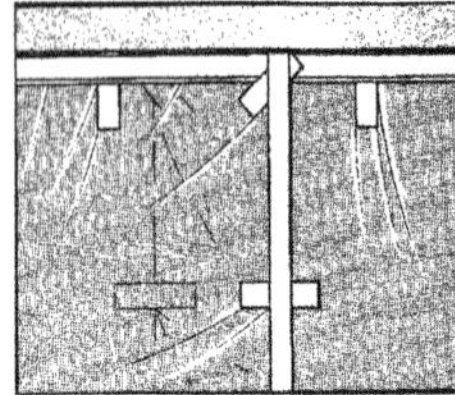

When you have finished putting the first layer of poly on the floor and walls, repeat steps 13 and 14 with a second layer. There must be two layers of poly on the floor and two on the walls. If there is a leak, the asbestos will get on the poly, not on the floor or walls.

Work areas can be poorly illuminated and confusing, especially in an emergency or in the dark. It is a good idea to make some arrows out of bright luminescent tape on the walls that point the way to the decon. In an emergency, the arrows will show you how to get out of the work area.

Testing the negative air machine

The negative air machine should pull the plastic flaps in the decon toward the machine. You can test the negative air pressure in the room. Puff ventilation smoke from outside the clean room into the work area. The air and smoke should be pulled in through the decon. The smoke should be sucked in, not drift out through cracks. Test the seals on primary barriers to make sure they are really airtight. (If you cut a hole to do the test, tape it up).

You have now built an airtight and watertight containment, which is under negative air pressure. You are ready to begin removing the asbestos.

SETUP

Key Facts

Good setup makes asbestos work safer and easier!

Always wear a suit and a respirator when you work with asbestos

1. Put up warning signs and barriers at eye level.
2. Shut off and isolate the ventilation system.
3. Shut off the electrical system. Lock out the electrical box. Don' t count on a switch to protect you.
4. Tape extension cords up off the floor.
5. Bring scaffolds and tools into the room before you build the decon.
6. The decon has three rooms (starting from the workroom):

Work room - Dirty room - Shower - Clean room

7. Set up the negative air machine at the other end of the room from the decon.
8. Clean everything in the room before you put up poly.
9. If you can' t clean somthing, wrap it in poly, label it, and take it to an asbestos landfill.
10. Take out anything you can move.
11. If you can' t take something out of the work area seal it airtight and water tight with poly and duct tape.
12. Cover all doors and windows with 2 layers of 6 mil poly. Cover air vents, pipe chases, and electrical outlets with 2 layers of 6 mil poly.
13. Tape one layer of poly on the floor, going up the walls one foot. Tape the edges of the poly to the walls.
14. Put one layer of 6 mil poly on the walls, coming down onto the floor one foot. Tape the edges of the poly to the floor. Put another layer of 6 mil poly on the floor and the walls.

Discussion questions

1. Why shouldn' t the electricity be turned off at the wall switches?
2. Why are two layers of poly put on the floor?
3. Some state laws say you have to put plywood on the floor if you leave carpets on the floor when you remove asbestos. Why is this done?
4. You have to protect yourself from asbestos when you set up. What other dangers do you need to think about when you' re setting up?
5. You are about to start a project where the material being removed is on the ceiling of a computer room and the computers cannot be shut down. How could you do the preparation of the work area?

For more information

*OSHA Asbestos Standard 29 CFR 1926.1101

* Chapter VI, "Pre-Work Activities and Considerations" and "Preparing the Work Area and Establishing the Decontamination Unit," in "Model Curriculum for Training Asbestos Abatement Contractors and Supervisors."

*EPA, "Guidance For Controlling Asbestos-Containing Materials in Buildings," (The Purple Book) EPA Publication No. EPA560/5-85-024.

*National Institute of Building Sciences, "Temporary Enclosures," in Model Asbestos Abatement Guide Specification, Section 01526.

***Your instructor may have a copy of this publication for you to look at.**

CHAPTER 7

REMOVAL

In this chapter you will learn:

How to go into the work room.
How to take asbestos off ceilings, walls, and pipes.
How to keep asbestos out of the air.
How to bag asbestos waste.
How to go out of the work room.
How your employer measures asbestos in the air.

Removal

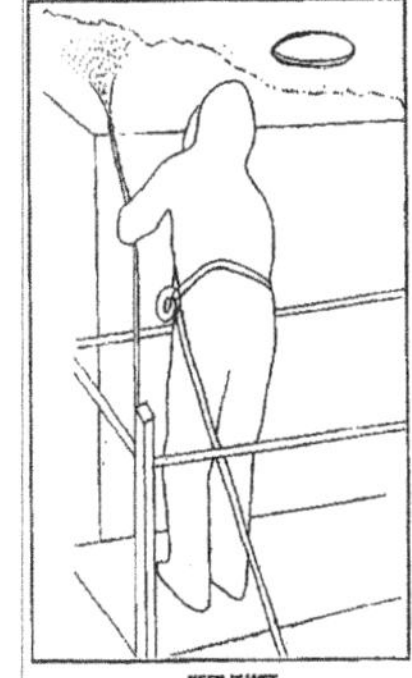

Six basic rules for working with asbestos:

- Keep the asbestos wet

- Contain the work area

- Filter the air

- Use negative pressure

- Practice good housekeeping

- Properly dispose of asbestos waste material

Good setup makes the work of taking asbestos off the substrate much easier. **Taking off asbestos safely means using the basic rules we' ve talked about all through this manual. You have to keep the asbestos wet, contain the work area, filter the air, use negative air pressure, practice good housekeeping, and properly cleanup and dispose of all waste. You also have to use respirators that fit right and disposable suits.**

Entering the work area

When you go into the work area, start in the clean room of the decon. In the clean room, take your street clothes off. Put them in a locker. **Inspect your respirator. Put it on and do the negative and positive pressure user seal checks. Make sure your respirator fits.**

Inspect your suit and put it on. Use duct tape to make it fit right so you won't trip over it. Pull the hood of the suit <u>over</u> the respirator straps. Tighten the hood around your face.

Always wear a respirator and a disposable suit when you work with asbestos.

Walk through the shower room and into the dirty (equipment) room. **Put on any gear stored there.** You might put on boots, hard hats, or a belt for your respirator hose. Pick up scrapers, squeegees, and other tools. If you are using a Type C respirator, the hookup is usually in the decon.

Some workers may put on pumps. These are called personal air sampling pumps. They are small air pumps that you wear on your belt. A hose goes under your shoulder. A small plastic cylinder with a paper filter clips to your collar. The filter faces down. The pump pulls air through the filter. The pump should be on all the time you are working. Asbestos in the air is caught on the filter. Your employer sends the filter to a lab. The lab tells him how many fibers are in the air when you are working.

Never touch the filter when you are working. This will interfere with the air sample. Personal air sampling tells you how much asbestos is in the air. The supervisor is responsible for deciding whether PAPR or Airline respirators will be worn. When there is more asbestos in the air, you have to wear a respirator with a higher Protection Factor.

When you go into the work area, the negative air machine should be on.

1. Keep the asbestos wet

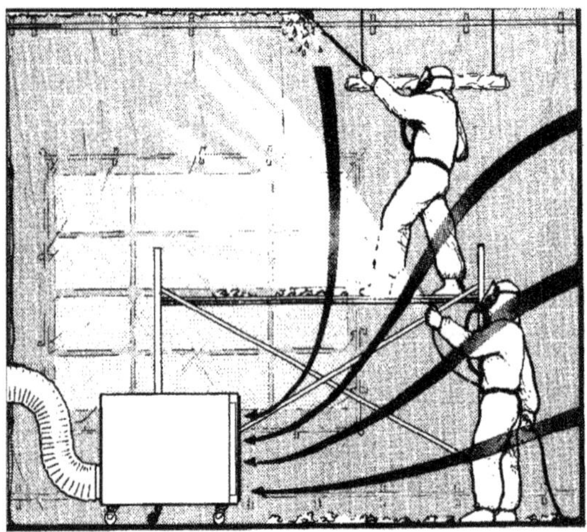

The first step in taking off the asbestos is getting it wet. Wet the asbestos before you remove it, while you remove it, and after you remove it. Use a low-pressure sprayer or a garden sprayer. Use enough amended water (water with surfactant) to really soak the asbestos. Follow the manufacturer's instructions when mixing the surfactant.

It may turn a darker color or swell a bit. Sometimes asbestos is in a paper cover. Make a small hole in the paper and spray water inside it.

At least one worker should wet the asbestos as the work goes on. He or she should make sure that the asbestos on the ceilings, pipes, etc. is really wet. The worker should mist the air as the work goes on. Drops of water will catch the asbestos in the air and pull it down to the floor. The worker should wet the asbestos on the floor until it is put in bags. Don' t use too much water. The work area should be damp, not flooded. If you use too much water it will make puddles on the floor. The water could leak through the poly or make someone slip. Remember that plain water will not soak into amosite asbestos. **Never use water on or around live electrical lines. You could get a bad shock. All temporary lines should be connected to a GFCI. Never use water on a hot steam line. The water could boil (flash) and burn you.**

2. Scraping

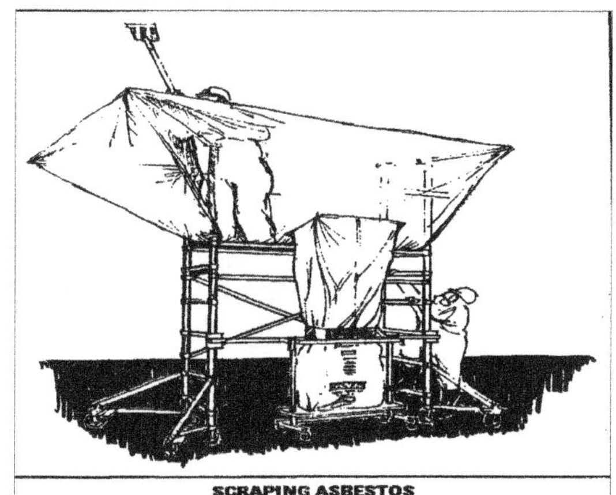

SCRAPING ASBESTOS

Once the asbestos is wet, it is usually the texture of cooked oatmeal. You can easily scrape it off with plastic or rubber scrapers. You may have to use ladders, scaffolds, or long handled scrapers to get to the asbestos. It is safer to use a scraper with a long handle though, than to stand on a scaffold.

Take asbestos off pipes with scrapers and utility knives. You may need snips to cut wire or metal bands. Chicken wire can be sharp. Use the tool to cut the metal. You can burn yourself on a hot pipe. Wear gloves to protect your hands. Asbestos may be in wire lath, which is heavy and sharp. You may need a hardhat or steel-toed boots to protect you from falling plaster. As you take asbestos off, don' t throw it. Don' t drop it. Scrape as much as you can directly into a waste bag to avoid cleaning up asbestos off the floor. If you work on a high ceiling, bag the asbestos on the scaffold or lower it to the ground using a scaffunnel (as in the picture). You must never use an air gun to blow asbestos off. Scrape it or cut it off.

Air samples show that air guns blow a lot of asbestos into the air. High-pressure water or air can force asbestos into cracks or blow it out of the work area. **Water guns cannot be used in Maryland.**

After you scrape off the big pieces, there will still be some asbestos on the substrate. Use a **nylon** brush to take off all the asbestos. **Wire brushes break the asbestos into smaller, more dangerous fibers.** Be sure to scrub off all the asbestos. Wipe the surface with a damp lint free rag until you can' t see any asbestos at all. Again, remember to keep folding the damp rag to expose a clean portion of the rag.

3. Bagging

Bagging asbestos promptly, as it is being removed, is one of the best ways to keep it out of the air and from accumulating on the floor. **The asbestos will dry out if it sits on the floor or piles up. When workers walk through it, a lot of asbestos will get in the air.** A few workers will use plastic shovels and squeegees to bag the asbestos as it is taken off. (Metal shovels can rip the poly). Be sure the asbestos is wet when you put it in the bag.

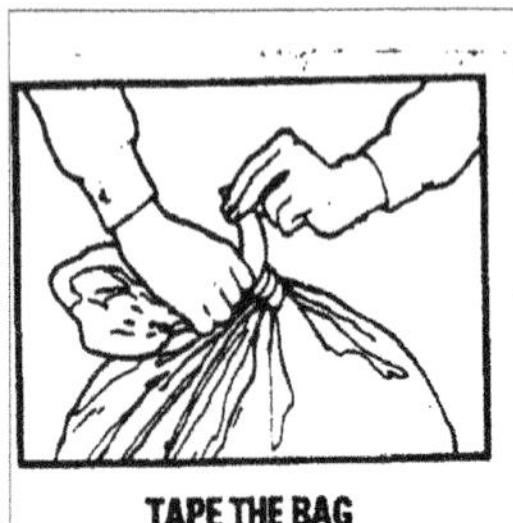

TAPE THE BAG

GOOSENECK THE BAG

Asbestos must be put in sealed containers (bags or drums) with warning labels. Use a HEPA vacuum to pull the air out of the bag. Then twist the top of the bag. Tape around it. Double the top of the bag back on itself. Tape around it again. This is called "goosenecking" the bag. Just tying a knot in the top of the bag will not make a water tight seal. On the job, workers usually put one bag inside another. If the first bag breaks, asbestos won' t leak out. This is called **double bagging**. Put sharp metal lath in cardboard drums. Wrap large pieces of waste (like carpets) in two layers of poly and tape them up. Put a label on the poly.

Only use the amount of water necessary to keep the asbestos wet so that workers won' t slip. Use a wet/dry HEPA vacuum to pick up small amounts of asbestos and water. (Water will ruin a dry HEPA vacuum).

4. Tools

Use plastic or wood tools, such as scrapers, shovels, and squeegees. Metal tools can rip the poly and can also contribute to electric shocks.

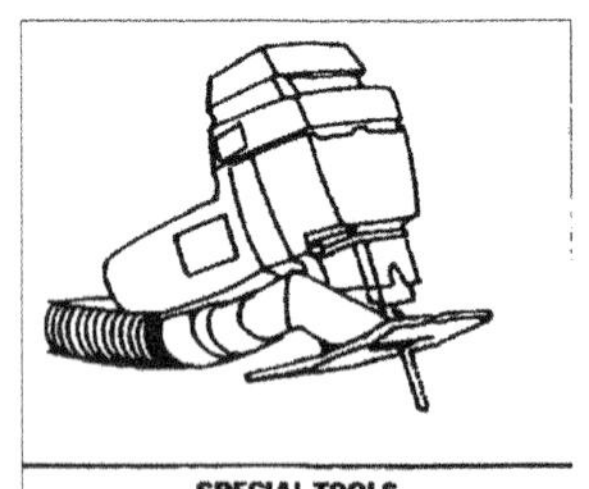

SPECIAL TOOLS

Use special power tools on an asbestos job. They have a HEPA vacuum attached. (This is called local ventilation or local exhaust ventilation). Power tools should be double insulated or they should be grounded. This means they are less likely to shock you, even if they are wet. **Never use a regular shop vacuum.** You should not use a regular drill, saw, or other power tool. All tools should have HEPA vacuums attached to them. Filters in the negative air machine need to be changed many times a day. Be sure they are wet before you put them in a waste bag.

Never take off your respirator inside the work area.

Always wear your respirator and disposable suit inside the work area. **Never take off your respirator inside the work area.** If your suit tears, fix it with duct tape. If you have to put on a new suit, you must decontaminate first (See page **145**)**. You may not eat, drink, chew gum, chew tobacco, smoke, or apply cosmetics in the work area.** To do that, you would have to take your respirator off. **Don' t do it!**

DON'T TAKE OFF YOUR RESPIRATOR

5. Clean up every day

Clean all of the asbestos off the floor at the end of every day. **Never allow the asbestos material to dry out.** Use wet rags and HEPA vacuums to clean the poly. It is easy to rip poly. Shovels, scaffolds, equipment, and tools can all rip the poly on the floor. A supervisor must check the poly periodically throughout the work and fix any rips or holes right away.

6. Decontamination

You must go through decontamination every time you leave the work area.

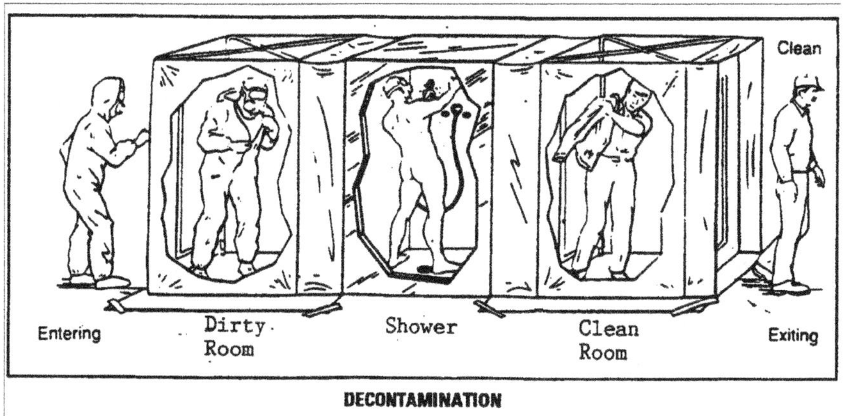

DECONTAMINATION

Before you leave the work area, clean off your suit and respirator by wet wiping or HEPA vacuuming them. In the decon take off your suit, take a shower, and wash your respirator. Leave the asbestos behind you.

In the work area, clean off your suit with a damp rag or a HEPA vacuum cleaner. Go into the dirty room (this is sometimes called the equipment room). Take off your hard hat, boots, and any other dirty equipment. Have your supervisor take off the sampling pump and turn it off. Wipe off your equipment and leave it in the dirty room.

Take off your suit carefully and discard it. Fold it inside out as you take it off. Try to keep the asbestos on the suit and off your skin. **Leave your respirator on, and get into the shower.** Wet wipe the motor and battery of the PAPR. **Do NOT get them wet.** Hold them away from the water. (A face mounted motor may need to be removed from the facepiece before showering) Wash off the facepiece of your respirator under the showerhead. Rinse your face and the rest of your body. Take the dirty wet filters off your respirator and throw them out. You can also put tape on the outside of the filters and put them in a bag. Remember water destroys HEPA filters. If your filters get wet, you must discard them. Take off your respirator and wash it in soap and water. Wash your body and your hair with soap and water. In the clean room, put on street clothes or another disposable suit. **It usually takes 3 to 5 minutes to decontaminate. If you do not take this long, you are probably taking asbestos home with you.** Don' t take asbestos fibers home, decontaminate every time you leave the work area!

The shower must have warm water, towels, and soap. There must be one shower for every ten workers. If men and women both work on the job, they will shower separately. **You must decontaminate every time you leave the work area.** Every time you take a break, you decontaminate. Every time you go to the bathroom, wash your face, eat, drink, or smoke, you must decontaminate. You must dispose of your suit, wash your respirator, and take a shower. On the way back in, you have to put on another suit. **You can' t take short cuts with decontamination.** You may decontaminate four or more times each day. At the end of the day, clean the dirty room. Use wet rags and HEPA vacuums. Clean up any asbestos you can see. Seal up the bag with dirty suits and respirator filters. Water from the shower must be filtered before going into the sewer system.

8. Asbestos cleanup jobs

Most asbestos jobs are planned ahead of time. But sometimes you may work on a job that wasn' t planned. If there is an accident - a fire, or a flood or a ceiling falls in - you may have to go and clean up the asbestos. The building owner has to shut off the ventilation and electricity as soon as the accident happens. The building owner must also get people out of the area and put up OSHA signs to keep non-asbestos workers out.

If you clean up such a site, you can' t just walk in and put up poly. You have to make sure the building is structurally safe to work in while you take out the asbestos. (A local government building code inspector must decide this) Is the electricity shut off? Is the fire totally out? Once you are sure the building is safe you can think about the asbestos.

After you set up, the job will, look like any other removal job. You will have to put up plastic, build a decon, and run a negative air machine. You must wear a respirator and a disposable suit. There may be a lot of asbestos in the air. You should wear a Type C respirator until air sampling shows that fiber levels are below 10f/cc.

When you come in, there will probably be dry asbestos all over the floor. Everyone must wear suits and respirators while setting up. Build the decon before you handle any asbestos. The first step is to get the asbestos wet. Bag some of the asbestos to make room to walk around in. Cover the air vents and set up a negative air machine. You may have to build barriers if the room opens up into a hallway. After that, take out the asbestos, just like any other job. If you are already on the job and a lot of asbestos falls down, get it wet right away. Stop all other work and bag up the asbestos.

9. The competent person

One of the most important people on an asbestos job is the "competent person". By **law, your employer has to have one person on every shift who makes sure that rules are followed.** The competent person is usually an accredited project designer or a supervisor who has been accredited under the Model Accreditation Plan. This person has 3 to 5 days of training respectively.

The competent person must make sure that no one but trained workers are on the job. The competent person must make sure that everyone wears respirators and suits. This person must make sure that there are enough suits, duct tape, respirator filters, and other supplies.

The competent person must supervise set up. The competent person must make sure that the negative air machine is working. The competent person must check the work room to make sure the poly stays up. He or she must make sure that everyone goes through decontamination. This person must make sure that rules about eating, drinking, and smoking on the job are followed. The competent person should be well trained, and a good source of information.

You should feel free to ask questions of your competent person about how to do the work safely. He or she should be able to answer them or know where to get the answers.

10. What you can do to work safely

There are many things your employer has to do to make the work safer. **But there are also a lot of things you have to do to keep yourself safe.** Always wear your respirator. Keep it in good shape. Do your fit checks. Wear your disposable suit and a hard hat if you need one. Clean yourself off carefully in the decon. Don' t take asbestos home with you. You are the only one who can do these things. **The difference between doing a good job and doing a sloppy job could cost you your health.**

11. Waste Disposal

You may only store 20 cubic yards of asbestos waste at your facility. Such waste must be in rigid containers (like fiber drums) inside a locked area. The containers of waste must be properly labeled. All waste that is disposed of must have a manifest. This manifest must be returned to the facility after the waste is disposed of.

REMOVAL

Key Facts

Good setup makes asbestos work easier and safer!

Protection

Use good work methods - keep the asbestos wet, contain the work area, use negative air pressure, filter the air with HEPA filters, and practice good housekeeping.
Use respirators that fit right and disposable suits.
Do negative and positive pressure user seal checks before you go in the work area.
Never take your respirator off inside the work area.

Removal

Wet the asbestos and keep it wet.
Do not use vacuum cleaners or power tools unless they have HEPA filters on them.
Do not drop or throw asbestos.
Bag it as you remove it as close to the removal area as possible
Keep asbestos out of the air by misting the air.

Waste disposal

Keep asbestos out of the air by bagging it as soon as possible while it is still wet.
Do not let the asbestos dry out.
Use waste bags with warning labels. Pull all the air out of the bag with a HEPA vacuum and seal it air tight. (Gooseneck the bag.)
No more than 20 cu. yds. can be stored at the facility.
Waste must have a manifest.

Decontamination

Enter and leave through the decon.
You must decontaminate yourself (throw out your suit, take a shower with your respirator on, and throw out your respirator filters) every time you leave the work room.

Setup and decon exercise

This is not a test. It is an exercise. Use it to see for yourself how well you understand the material in the chapter.

1. Why do you contain the work area?

2. How do you do it?

3. In what order do you cover the work area with poly?

4. Where is the equipment room?

5. What happens in the equipment room?

Discussion questions

1. Why do you put colored chalk under the seams between sheets of poly on the floor?

2. Why do you put tape or wood over poly on stairs in the work area?

3. There are some jobs where you need to be extra careful. If you know about good work methods, how to wear a respirator, and how to understand air-sampling results, you can figure out what to do on an unusual job. Here are a few examples which you can use for discussion:

   Amosite asbestos
   Can' t shut off electricity
   Working equipment in the room
   Taking off asbestos above a dropped ceiling
   Taking off part of the asbestos in a large room (taking off half of the ceiling from a whole warehouse)

For more information

*OSHA Asbestos Standard 29 CFR 1926.1101

*Chapter XI. "Confining and Minimizing Airborne Fibers," in "Model curriculum for Training Asbestos Abatement Contractors and Supervisors."

*EPA, "Guidance for Controlling Asbestos-Containing Materials in Buildings," (the "Purple Book"), EPA Publication No. EPA 560/5-85-024.

*National Institute of Building Sciences, "Removal of Asbestos-Containing Materials," in Model Asbestos Abatement Guide Specifications, Section 02081.

***Your instructor may have a copy of these publications for you to look at.**

CLEANUP AND DISPOSAL

In this chapter you will learn:

How to clean up the work area.
How to take down the poly on the walls and floor.
What happens to asbestos after it leaves the job.
How your employer tests the air at the end of the job.
How to replace the insulation

Cleanup and disposal

Clean up all the asbestos you can see ... and all the asbestos fibers you can' t see

It is very important to clean up the work area after you remove the asbestos. The work is not finished until it passes a final visual inspection by the competent person (supervisor) and an air sample test. These are very strict tests. If all of the asbestos has not been cleaned off the beams, poly, waste bags, pipes, and other surfaces, the job will not pass them. Everything will have to be cleaned again, until the job passes theses tests. It can be very expensive to clean and take air samples again. If you do a careful job the first time, you will not have to spend time later on cleaning the room again.

1. Clean up the asbestos you can see

It takes a long time to clean up an asbestos job. The first step is to clean up all the asbestos you can see. As you take the asbestos down, bag it up. Clean the substrate and other surfaces with a nylon bristle brush. Wipe the surface with a damp lint free rag until you can' t see any fibers. Be sure to fold over the rag to get a clean surface each time or you will re-contaminate areas. A supervisor will do a visual inspection at this time to ensure that no visible asbestos remains on the substrate. Next, remove any bags of asbestos waste from the work area. Make sure you wipe them off first.

2. Waste disposal

Everything used on the job must be cleaned or disposed of.

Poly, disposable suits, and respirator filters have to be disposed of with the asbestos. All poly has to be sealed in airtight bags with labels just like asbestos. Sometimes there is a waste load out chamber, which is like a decon for waste bags. It has two rooms - a wash room and a holding room. A worker inside the work area puts the bag into the wash room. A worker in the wash room washes off the bag and stores it in the holding room. People don' t walk through the waste-load-out. Only waste bags go through it.

Anything with asbestos on it must be taken to a landfill that follows EPA regulations. It must be sealed in leak-proof, labeled bags or containers. The waste truck must have closed sides and a top and lockable doors. The truck should be lined with poly. It must be cleaned at the end of the job.

3. Take down the first layer of poly

After you have locked down the substrate, you are ready to wet wipe and HEPA vacuum the first layer of poly. Use lint free rags to do the wiping so that they won't leave fibers behind. Some air clearance methods can't distinguish between rag fibers and asbestos fibers. Also, wipe in one direction only and never go back over an area you just wiped. Start at the top and work down. Fold the rag frequently to expose a clean surface. After the first cleaning, do an inspection. Make sure there is no asbestos that can be seen. After you clean, you' re ready to take down the first layer of poly.

Start with the wall poly and then do the floor poly. Cut the sheets into three to six-foot-wide strips. Cut through one layer of poly only. **Gently** loosen the duct tape. Roll the poly onto itself, from the top down. Fold it into bundles that you can handle easily, and bag it.

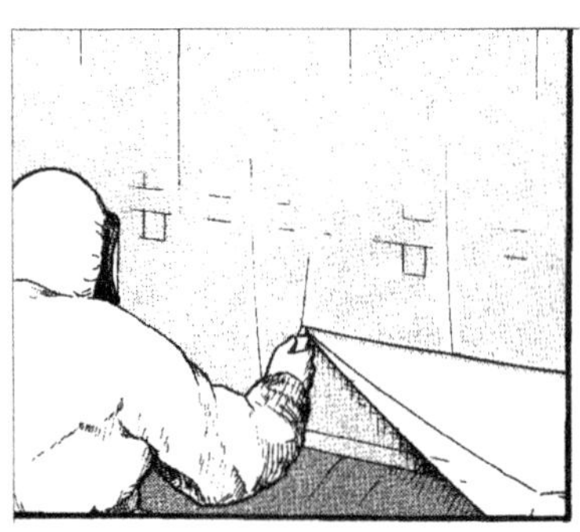

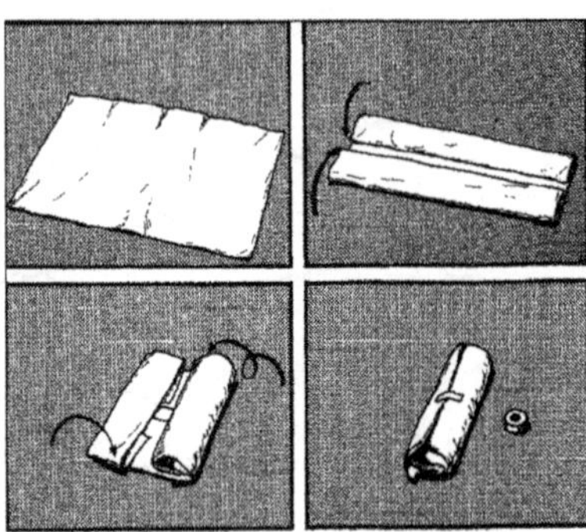

4. Take down the second layer of poly

Repeat the actions in step 3 for the second layer of poly. Remember to allow time for a visual inspection before removing the poly.

5. Take the poly off non -moveable objects/ clean poly on critical barriers

Clean the poly on the non-moveable objects just as you did for the first and second layers of poly. Remove this poly after you make sure it is cleaned. Next, clean the poly on the critical barriers but **do not** remove it. This poly must remain in place until the job passes final air clearance monitoring. (On most Level II jobs, final clearance air monitoring will not be necessary. In this case you can remove the critical barrier poly after you remove the poly from the non-moveable objects.)

6. Shut off negative air machine(s)/Disassemble the Decon

After the job passes the air monitoring, you can shut off the negative air machines and disassemble the decon. The negative air machines, tools, and the interior of the decon should have been cleaned prior to this. Take apart the decon in pieces and roll the poly in on itself. Plywood must be disposed of as contaminated waste but PVC pipe can be cleaned and reused.

If you are putting back a substitute material, you can leave the critical barrier poly and the decon in place until you have put up the substitute material.

7. Tool Clean-up

Cleaning tools

Everything that leaves the job has to be cleaned. This includes:

scrapers	respirator	scaffolds	hoses
squeegees	hard hats	ladders	tools
water sprayers	boots	negative air machines	
HEPA vacuums			

Scrub everything off and rinse it well. Seal it in clear waste bags with labels, and take to the next job. You must clean everything very well, especially if it will be used on a non-asbestos job.

CLEANUP AND DISPOSAL

Key Facts

1. **Use damp lint free rags and HEPA vacuums to clean up the work area.**

   First clean all the asbestos you can see.
   Then clean all the asbestos you can' t see.

2. **Spray a lockdown encapsulant on the surface and on the poly.**

3. **Roll up the poly from the top down and bag it as asbestos waste.**

   Leave the critical barriers in place until the job passes the clearance air sampling.

4. **Take asbestos, poly, dirty suits and other waste to an EPA-approved asbestos landfill.**

5. **Clean all tools with wet rags and HEPA vacuums.**

6. **The clearance air sampling tells the building owner whether the area is clean enough.**

   Clearance air sampling uses aggressive sampling - stirring up the air with fans and leaf blowers.

   Clearance air samples are sent to a lab, where the fibers are counted. A Transmission Electron Microscope (TEM) is often used.

   A job is not clean until air-sampling results show less than .01 f/cc or background.

7. **After the job passes the clearance air sampling, put on new insulation (sprayback) and take down critical barriers.**

Discussion Questions

1. Why is it important to clean up the poly if it will be thrown away?
2. Some people say that lockdown should not be used. They argue that cleanup should be done so well that lockdown is not needed. What do you think?
3. After taking off most of the asbestos, a contractor spray painted the beams instead of cleaning them off. What is the problem with this?
4. Why is the air stirred up before clearance air samples are taken?
5. Why do you wait until after the job passes the air test to put on sprayback?
6. In what order would you conduct the following clean-up activities?

   _____ Wet wipe/HEPA vacuum first layer of plastic.
   _____ Conduct **final** visual inspection of the work area.
   _____ Disassemble the decontamination unit.
   _____ Wet wipe/HEPA vacuum the second layer of plastic.
   _____ Clean critical barriers.
   _____ Conduct clearance air monitoring.
   _____ Take down critical barriers.
   _____ Spray a lockdown encapsulant on substrate.
   _____ Remove all bags of ACM debris from the work area.

FOR MORE INFORMATION

*OSHA Asbestos Standard, 29 CFR 1926.1101

* Chapter IV. "Sampling and Analytical Methodology Pertaining to Asbestos Abatement," in "Model Curriculum for Training Asbestos Abatement Contractors and Supervisors."

* EPA, "Asbestos Waste Management Guidance: Generation, Transport, Disposal," Publication No. EPA/530-SW-85-007.

Your instructor may have a copy of these publications for you to look at.

Lock down the asbestos fibers you can' t see

Once a visual inspection by a competent person verifies that there is no visible residue, seal up the asbestos fibers you can' t see. Use a low-pressure sprayer to spray a sealant called "lockdown". You can spray or brush apply the sealant to pipes. Be sure that the "lockdown" you use is compatible with the substrate to which it is applied and the new insulation that will be installed. The "lockdown" glues down any fibers you missed so they can' t get in the air. It is hard to pass the air sample clearance test at the end of the job without it. You may not use lockdown spray instead of cleaning.

Sprayback or Replace the Asbestos Containing Material with Non-Asbestos Containing Material

Many times new insulation to replace the asbestos is needed. This could be fiberglass, mineral wool, or some other non-asbestos insulation. This replacement is called sprayback. Don' t put up sprayback or replacement until the job passes the final visual inspection and the final clearance air test. Replacement materials may not be completely safe! Find out how to work safely with them. You should wear a respirator when you put up fiberglass or mineral wool. Just because the material isn' t asbestos, doesn' t mean it' s safe. After you put up the sprayback or replacement material, you can take down the critical barriers. You can take the poly off the objects in the room. You can clean the decon and take it down. You can take out the negative air machine. Sprayback or replacement material must meet the requirements of applicable building codes.

Air Sampling

Your employer must take 8-hour air samples from some workers on every shift. **(There are a few exceptions).** Your employer has to know how much asbestos is in the air under the worst conditions. Usually, 1/4 of the workers wear sampling pumps each day.

Personal air samples also tell you whether you' re doing the work right (keeping asbestos out of the air). If air samples show a lot of asbestos in the air, you should be sure that the asbestos is really wet, that the negative air machine is working, and that asbestos isn' t piling up on the floor.

Building owners sometimes take air samples **outside** the work area. They want to know if asbestos is leaking out of the work area. These are called **area air samples.**

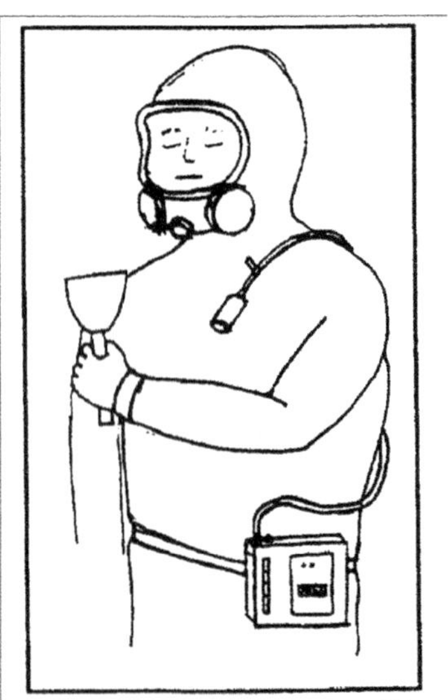
TAKING PERSONAL AIR SAMPLE

You may see air-sampling pumps outside the clean room. You may also see them outside the negative air machine or outside the building. **Even if your employer takes <u>area</u> air samples, the employer also has to sample workers.**

At the end of the day the filters from the air sampling pumps go to a lab. At the lab, the technician cuts a small piece of the filter. The technician dissolves the filter and counts the asbestos fibers under a microscope. The microscope is called a **Phase Contrast Microscope (PCM).** The lab sends your employer a report. The report has the number of asbestos fibers per cubic centimeter of air (fibers per cc or f/cc). **Your employer must post the air sampling results as soon as he or she gets them from the lab.**

Air Sample Results Help To:

1. **Tell if you are using the right respirator.**

2. **Tell if your work practices are working.**

Testing the air at the end of the job

Prior to testing the air, a final visual inspection is done by the owner's representative and the competent person. All visible residue must be cleaned up before clearance air testing. A job may look clean, but what about the asbestos you can' t see? There is no way to know if the room is clean without testing the air. On some jobs, after the poly is taken down, an industrial hygienist (IH) will take air samples. The air samples tell the building owner whether the room is clean enough.

This final air sampling is called clearance air sampling. Clearance air sampling is different from the air samples taken on workers. The air is stirred up with fans and leaf blowers. A pump pulls air through a filter. The fans stir up any fibers that are on the walls, floors, or corners. More fibers can be caught on the filter. Stirring up the air in this manner is called aggressive sampling.

The final air sample is sent to a lab, where the filters are counted. There are several ways to count the fibers. In many cases, the area is considered clean enough when an air sample is less than .01 (point oh one) fibers per cc. Sometimes the

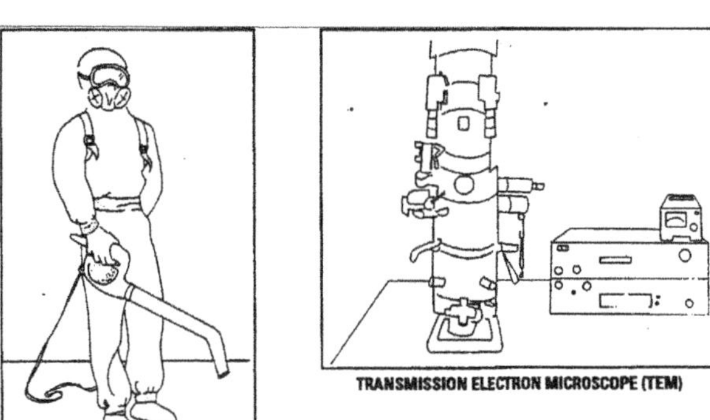

AGGRESSIVE SAMPLING WITH A LEAF BLOWER

TRANSMISSION ELECTRON MICROSCOPE (TEM)

area is clean enough when it is at least as clean as the air outside the area. For schools, the lab usually uses a very powerful microscope called a Transmission Electron Microscope (TEM).

Remember that the job isn't done until the final air clearance test is passed.

If the job does not pass the clearance air sampling, the area must be cleaned again. This is why critical barriers are left up until the job passes the test.

Chapter 9

OTHER HEALTH AND SAFETY PROBLEMS

In this chapter you will learn about these dangers on asbestos jobs:

Problems with heat.
Chemicals.
Electrical shocks.
Fires.
Confined spaces.
Dangers from scaffolds and ladders.
Slips, trips, and falls.

Safety

Asbestos is a slow danger on a removal job. But **short-term hazards, such as electrocution and fires, can hurt you much more quickly**. Asbestos removal is demolition work. Demolition is the most dangerous type of construction work. Here are some of the short-term dangers on asbestos jobs:

1. Heat stroke, heat exhaustion, and heat cramps
2. Chemicals other than asbestos
3. Electrical shocks
4. Fires and explosions
5. Confined spaces
6. Dangers from scaffolds and ladders
7. Slips, trips, and falls

Heat

Your body tries to cool itself by sweating and the evaporation of sweat. On the job, you work in a suit that doesn' t let your body heat escape and evaporation of sweat cannot take place. Your lungs have to work harder to pull air through a respirator. The air conditioning must be shut off. You work very hard. If your body overheats, you can get very sick. Overheating can cause **heat cramps, heat exhaustion,** or **heat stroke** (a medical emergency).

Heat stroke happens when your body can' t control its temperature. You stop sweating. Sweating is the main way your body cools itself. Your body overheats. **Heat stroke can kill you or cause permanent brain damage.**

Here are some signs of heat stroke:

hot skin
headache
dry skin
dizziness
flushed skin
nauseous (feel sick to stomach)
confusion
fainting
elevated core body temperature

Heat stroke is a medical emergency!

If a worker shows signs of heat stroke, get the person to the hospital right away. Unless the victim is treated quickly, he or she could die. Call an ambulance. Until the ambulance comes, you need to cool the person. Get the worker out of the work area and into a cooler location. (Due to the life threatening nature of the emergency, decon takes a back seat). Take off the suit and respirator. Be sure that the person is still breathing. Fan the person. **DO NOT COOL THE PERSON WITH COLD WATER!** You could cause them to go into shock and worsen their condition. Also, **Do not attempt to give water to drink to a person who is unconscious. You could cause them to choke.**

Heat exhaustion is less serious than heat stroke. Heat exhaustion happens when you lose a lot of water from sweating. Sometimes you lose a lot of salt, too. **Here are some signs of heat exhaustion:**

cool clammy skin
headache
sweaty skin
dizziness
pale skin
nauseous (feel sick to stomach)
a feeling of weakness

Do these sound familiar? The last three signs of heat exhaustion: headache, dizzy, and nauseous are also signs of heat stroke? If a worker has hot, dry, flushed skin, he or she probably has heat stroke - get the person to the hospital. If the person has cool, clammy, pale skin, he or she probably has heat exhaustion. Get the worker out of the work room and into a cooler area. Take off the suit and respirator and give the person cool (**NOT COLD**) water to drink. If the worker faints, call an ambulance. He or she may have heat stroke. **Do not give water to drink to a person is unconscious. You may cause them to choke.**

Watch out for these warning signs of a person being over-come by heat:

- **less alert**
- **less coordinated**
- **gets a headache**
- **feels sick to stomach**

This could be the beginning of heat stroke or heat stress. Get the person out of the work area and into a cooler area. Heat can make you less coordinated, and this can cause other accidents. Heat can also cause muscle cramps or heat rash. These are uncomfortable, but they are not serious. Heat can also make a worker faint. Take the worker out of the work area. Be sure that a person who is unconscious does not have a more serious problem.

Preventing heat problems

Take breaks and drink water to prevent problems with heat!

Here are some ways to prevent heat problems:

Drink lots of water - Your body loses lots of water when you sweat. It is best to drink every half-hour in an uncontaminated area (outside work area). But you probably won' t be able to go through the decon that often. Drink 8 to 16 ounces of water at every break. (Sometimes sports drinks can be helpful).

Drink some orange juice or eat bananas. Or eat potato chips or **one** salty food once a day. Your body may need a little extra salt. But most Americans already eat too much salt. **If you are on a low-salt diet for your heart, do not eat extra salt. Salt tablets are very dangerous. Do not take them.**

Take breaks - Your body will handle heat better if it can cool down sometimes. At least two breaks a day and a lunch break will help your body handle heat better. You will need to go through proper decontamination procedures every time you take a break. Make sure that you go to a cooler area to take your break.

Get used to the heat gradually - It takes about two weeks for your body to get used to working in the heat. Your body can get unused to heat in about 4 days. New workers should only work a half-day in the heat for the first few days. They should not work a full shift until the end of their first work week.

Use cooling vests - There is some new equipment that can help keep you cool. Cooling vests have ice packs in them. When you are working in very hot areas, cool vests can prevent heat problems.

Cut down on alcohol - Alcohol dries out your body and can increase your body temperature. Even if you only have two beers the night before work, you are more likely to have problems with heat.

II. Chemicals other than Asbestos

An asbestos filter on your respirator will not protect you from other chemicals **You have learned about some dangerous chemicals used at work:**

surfactant (in amended water)
fiberglass (for replacing)
solvents (for taking off floor tile glue)
lockdown
encapsulants
carbon monoxide (from motors)

An asbestos filter on your respirator will not protect you from other chemicals. For any chemical you work with check with the manufacturer to determine which type of respiratory protection you will need. For example, you might need both a **black** filter (for an organic solvent) **and** a **purple** or **magenta** filter (for asbestos and fiberglass). You might need both a **green** filter (for ammonia) **and** a **purple** or **magenta** filter (for asbestos and fiberglass). Some of these combination filters are **gray**.

You may also remove asbestos some place where other chemicals are used. You need to know what you are working with. **Your employer must have you trained about the chemicals you work with (including their hazards and how to work with them safely).** This is called **Right - To - Know training.** **See SEC 4** for more about your right to know about chemicals.

Carbon Monoxide

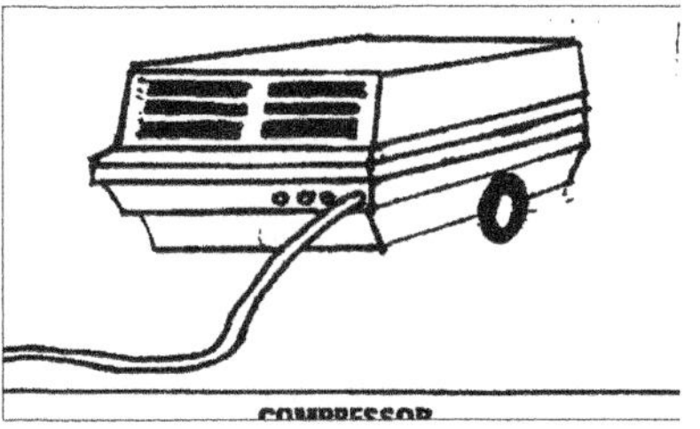

Carbon monoxide is a poisonous gas you can't see or smell.

Carbon monoxide is a dangerous gas. It can poison you. It can cause permanent brain damage and can even kill you. It has no smell, taste, or color. It comes from motors (engines), such as air compressors and generators. It can be a real problem if you are using Type C respirators. Here are some signs of carbon monoxide poisoning:

Suddenly you begin to feel drunk and dizzy and you may start swaying back and forth. Your thinking gets foggy. You may feel like you're coming down with the flu. You may even begin to act crazy and can fall unconscious. You may feel:

faint
headache
throw up
nauseous (sick to stomach)
sleepy
dizzy

Does this sound familiar? Three signs of carbon monoxide poisoning: headache, nausea, and dizziness are also signs of heat stroke and heat stress. If a worker has these signs, get them out of the work area and take off their respirator. If they faint, call an ambulance. If a person does not respond to you when you call their name and shake them, they are unconscious. If a worker becomes unconscious because of carbon monoxide poisoning, he/she may need CPR (cardio-pulmonary resuscitation). CPR is a way to get someone' s heart and lungs working again when the heart stops. There should always be someone on your crew who has CPR certification. Taking CPR classes can certify you.

If you begin to have signs of carbon monoxide poisoning and you are wearing a Type C respirator, turn on your escape gear and disconnect your airline. Alert your co-workers and get out of the work area. Help your co-workers to get out and have the air purification system checked. (This is why the State Employees Asbestos Program has recommended in the past that you use grade D bottled air instead of a gasoline-powered compressor).

III. Electrical shocks

An electric shock can stop your heart. Electricity is measured in **volts. Even a few volts can kill you if the electricity goes through your heart.** Electricity follows the easiest path - to the earth. It is very easy for electricity to travel through water. If you are wet and you touch electricity, it may travel through your body.

A wire with electricity going through it is called a "live" wire. If a tool or an extension cord is broken, it may have a **short.** This means that the electricity doesn' t flow through the right wires. It may flow through the tool and into your body.

Electricity is a problem on asbestos jobs for many reasons:

a lot of water is used
power may not be shut off
power tools are used
extension cords are used
metal tools may be used
wires are exposed when the asbestos is removed

Electricity and water are a deadly combination!

Water - Don' t use more water than you need to. Don' t use so much water that there are puddles on the floor. Clean up small amounts of water with a wet/dry HEPA vacuum. **Never use water around live wires or power tools.**

Shut off the power - Lock the electrical box. Your employer should have an electrician come in and test the wires. Never assume that the power has been shut off. You might think that all the power is shut off, but it may not be. You could be in for a big surprise.

Cover electrical outlets - Be sure that electrical outlets and boxes are covered watertight.

Use safe power tools - Power tools should be **double insulated**. This means the outside of the tool doesn' t touch the wires in the cord. Tools could also b**grounded.** This means there is an extra wire in the cord. If there is a **short**, electricity will travel through the extra wire. Electricity should not go into your body. A **grounded** tool has three prongs on the plug (instead of two.) **Never cut the third prong off a grounded plug.** Use an adapter. Attach the wire on the adapter to the plate on the outlet.

Keep power tools in perfect shape - It is much easier to get a shock from a broken tool. Broken tools should be taken off the job. They should have a DO NOT USE tag on them. Do not try to fix a broken tool unless you have been trained and authorized to do so. Always unplug a tool before trying to fix it. Some companies cut the cord of a broken tool so no one can use it.

Here are some ways to keep tools in perfect shape

inspect the tool before you use it
give broken tools to your supervisor to be taken out of service and repaired
be sure the tool is sharp - the motor has to work harder if it is dull
don' t carry a tool by its cord
don' t unplug a tool by pulling on the cord
store tools where they won' t be damaged

Use safe extension cords - Heavy-duty wire (i.e. romex) **is not** meant for temporary wiring. Your employer **must** give you extension cords with plugs for power tools. Your employer should give you grounded extension cords that are heavy duty and waterproof..

Keep extension cords in perfect shape - There may be a lot of extension cords on the job. The negative air machine or HEPA vacuum needs one. So do power tools and lights. Extension cords need to be taped up off of the floor. If a scaffold runs over the cords, it could cut them.

Never hang extension cords with wire. This could damage the insulation and cause a shock. When you attach a tool to an extension cord put electrical tape around the joint. Do this when you attach two extension cords together or tape them up on the wall.

Never use metal hand tools or ladders - Electricity travels through metal. If you touch a live wire with a metal shovel, you could get a bad shock. Your employer should give you plastic or other non-conductive tools. Metal tools with plastic handles are safer. Metal ladders are also dangerous. Your employer should give you fiberglass ladders.

Wires in walls or ceilings - When you scrape asbestos off a ceiling, you might uncover wires. It is very important to shut off the electricity, lock out the circuit, and have an electrician test it.

If a worker has been shocked, do not touch him. You might get a shock yourself. Shut off the power first. Then use a dry non-conductive pole to move the worker away from anything metal.

Someone on the job should be trained to do CPR. (CPR stands for Cardio - Pulmonary Resuscitation.) A person trained in CPR can keep someone breathing and keep his/her heart going until an ambulance comes. Do not try CPR unless you have been trained.

Preventing Electrical Shocks

Use Ground Fault Interrupters to prevent shocks

The best way to protect workers from shocks is to prevent shocks. OSHA says your employer has to prevent shocks. Your employer can use a sensitive **circuit breaker** or a **written program.** Using a GFCI is more effective than a written program.

A Ground Fault Circuit Interrupter (GFCI) is a very sensitive circuit breaker. If there is a short, the GFCI should shut off the power before it can hurt your heart. A Ground Fault Circuit Interrupter is a very good way to prevent shocks. Each extension cord should have its own GFCI.

Your employer can also use a **written program.** With a written program, you count on a person (instead of a piece of equipment) to keep you safe. **Written programs may not be a good way to protect workers from shocks!** Because of this the State Employees Program stresses the use of GFCI' s.

Protection

A competent person must also be knowledgeable in electrical safety and must supervise all work. Preventing shocks is the best way to protect yourself. It is essential to have all sources of electricity in the work area identified and locked out. Each worker should have their own lock and tag. (Procedures should follow OSHA's lockout/tagout standard). Circuit testing equipment is also necessary to ensure that the lines have been deactivated.

REMINDER: State Employees cannot do asbestos jobs where the electricity cannot be shut off.

IV. Fires and Explosions

Prevent fires: keep flames, sparks, and red hot surfaces out of the work area and the decon

A fire on an asbestos job is very dangerous. **Poly, duct tape, and disposable suits burn fast. Poly will melt and can burn at about 150 degrees. The negative air machine makes the fire spread faster. The work area can be dark and there is usually only one exit.**

The best way to deal with fires is to prevent them. Any fire needs three things: fuel (something that burns), heat (the heat, flames or spark that starts the fire), and oxygen (in the air).

Preventing fires means keeping fuel, heat, and oxygen from coming together.

FUEL	HEAT	OXYGEN
poly	welding	air
duct tape	cutting torches	negative air machine
plastics	electrical wires	
encapsulant	lights	
disposable suits	broken tools	
wood	operating machines	
solvents	cigarettes	

Welding and cutting - These are often used in demolition. If needed, this should only be done with the knowledge and approval of the Agency Safety & Health Specialist. A worker must stand by with a fire extinguisher in case any sparks fly.

Electrical wires and lights - An ordinary lamp on the floor can start a fire. Never wrap lights in poly. Heat will build up and can set the poly on fire. Your employer must use safety lights. The lights have cages that keep the hot bulb from starting a fire.

Tools - If tools are kept in perfect shape, they are not likely to start a fire.

Operating machines - These need extra protection during setup. For example machines with moving parts that will overheat when covered in plastic.

Do not smoke on the job!!

Cigarettes - These are not allowed on asbestos jobs. Do not smoke during setup. Poly and solvents both catch fire very easily.

There are some new products, which can help prevent fires. Fire-resistant poly doesn' t burn as easily. New chemicals that don' t burn as easily are available. However, both will still burn under the right conditions.

In case of Fire

Look at the escape plan when you start the job

If there is a fire in the work area or decon, <u>**GET OUT!**</u> The fire will spread very quickly. You may have to cut through the poly to get out of the work area or decon. Your employer must have a **fire extinguisher** and an **escape plan**. **Fire extinguishers** need to be able to put out wood, chemical, and electrical fires. These are called **ABC - type** fire extinguishers. Your Agency Safety & Health Specialist should be consulted to ensure that you have the right capacity rating for the job. If there are sprinklers, your employer should try to leave them in service as long as possible. The **escape plan** includes a map and emergency phone numbers. The plan should be hung both inside and outside the decon. When you start a job, look at the map. Figure out how you would get out in an emergency. Do you have to dial "9" to make a phone call outside of the building? Is there an emergency exit from the work area? Are there arrows made out of tape on the walls to show you how to get out? If the fire started near the decon, you will not be able to get out that way. Where is the fire extinguisher? Do you know how to use it? **Remember: In case of a fire emergency GET OUT, don't worry about decontamination.**

V. Confined Spaces

There are a few rare cases where you work in a small area that is hard to get out of. This might happen if you are taking asbestos off the inside of a steam tunnel, crawl space, trench, etc.. It is hard to get out of these **confined spaces**. They also may have very little oxygen in them. You can use up all of the oxygen in the space very quickly. Many people die in **confined spaces.** A **confined space** is define as a space that has a limited means of entry or exit, cannot achieve adequate dilution ventilation through natural or mechanical means, and can have an oxygen deficiency or an unsafe accumulation of toxic and/or combustible agents.

SELF-CONTAINING BREATHING APPARATUS (SCBA)

If you work inside of a confined space, you should wear either a **Self-Contained Breathing Apparatus (SCBA)** or an **Type C Airline respirator with at least a 5 to 15 min. escape tank of air if there is the possibility that the atmosphere could turn Immediately Dangerous to Life or Health.** You must wear a rescue harness assembly. There must be another worker outside who remains in constant communication with you all of the time. He can pull you out or get help if something goes wrong. There also must be adequate lighting and someone trained in CPR. No one should go into a confined space to rescue a worker unless he has been trained and is properly equipped. Many people die trying to rescue workers from confined spaces.

In addition, any utility or process line that contains a harmful agent which enters a confined space must be completely isolated from entering the confined space. All electrical service and equipment must be locked and tagged out of service. The atmosphere inside the confined space must first be tested for oxygen deficiency and **then** for toxic or combustible gases.

Under the OSHA confined space regulation (29 CFR 1910.146) some spaces require permits. These would include spaces which has the potential to contain a hazardous atmosphere, contains a material which could engulf a person who enters the space, has a configuration that could trap or asphyxiate a person, and/or contains other serious health or safety hazards.

Additional information can be found in the COMAR 09.12.35 and OSHA 29 CFR 1910.146 standards.

VI. Ladders

You already know not to use metal or wooden ladders. Electricity passes through them, and it can shock you. Also be sure that ladders are in perfect shape.

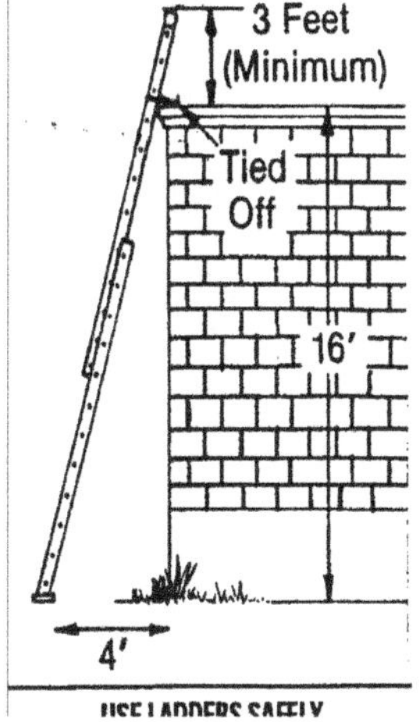

Every time you use a ladder, check for these deficiencies

broken rungs or steps
broken hinges
broken feet
wobbly ladder
no rubber safety feet
water on the ladder (slippery)

Here are some ways to use ladders safely:

Don't lean a stepladder against a wall. Use a ladder that' s made to lean against a wall. **If you lean a ladder against a wall, set it up so that the top of the ladder is four times higher than the distance from the wall to the base of the ladder.**

Only use one side of a stepladder. The other side isn' t made to hold a person.**Face the ladder.** Don' t stand on ibackwards. **Don' t stand higher than two steps from the top of a stepladder.** Get a taller ladder. **Don't use a ladder as a platform.**

VII. Scaffolds

Scaffolds on wheels are common on asbestos jobs.
All scaffolds should have guardrails!

You can' t tell whether a scaffold is safe by looking at it. Scaffolds must be put together by someone with experience. All the parts must fit perfectly. They should be inspected by someone other than the person who built them.

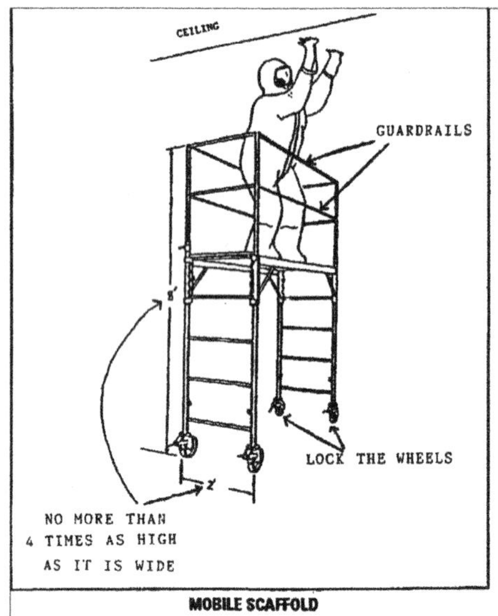

MOBILE SCAFFOLD

Here are some rules about scaffolds:

All scaffolds should have railings.
These keep you from falling over the side.

Scaffolds more than 10 feet high must have railings and toe boards

The scaffold parts must be locked together with pins

Manually propelled mobile scaffolds shall be provided with positive locking devices such as wheel brakes and locks, to hold the scaffold into position.

Scaffolds may not be more than 4 times higher than the minimum base dimension. For example, a 6 - foot wide scaffold may not be more than 24 feet high.

Platforms shall be tightly planked for the full width of the scaffold except for necessary entrance opening Platforms shall be secure in place. Boards shall extend over their end supports not less than 6 inches or more than 12 inches. Otherwise, if you step on the end of the board, the board could tip over and you would fall. It is safer to use scrapers with long handles than to work on a scaffold.

If you are using supplied air respirators, it is easy for the hose to be caught on the scaffold. Protect the hoses from damage. Be sure there is enough hose for you to move around. It is even more important not to fall off scaffolding. If you fall, the hose may trap you. It can pull the respirator off your face or knock you off balance. The hose could pull other people off the scaffold.

VIII. Slips, trips, and falls

When you work, you wear slippery booties on your feet, the floor has plastic on it, and there is water on the floor. This combination contributes to slips, trips, and falls. You may drag a 300-foot long air hose behind you. You could trip on the hose or it could get tangled. You could fall down and, for example, break your arm.

Here are some ways to prevent slips, trips, and falls on the job:

Don' t use more water than you need to keep the asbestos adequately wet. . Use a wet/dry HEPA vacuum to pick up small amounts of water.

When you set up the job make sure that the poly on the floor is as smooth and straight as possible

Clean up asbestos and other debris as you are working

Wear boots outside your booties. You cannot wear these boots outside an asbestos job.

Tape extension cords up on the walls

Keep boxes, bags, and other items out of the way

Keep airlines from getting tangled

Back Injuries

Don't fill bags more than one-third full

Back injuries are very common and very painful. They are hard to treat. It is much easier to prevent back problems than to treat them.

Here are some ways to prevent back problems:

Don' t fill bagsmore than 1/3 full.

Figure out how much you can comfortably lift.

Figure out a way to lift that' s comfortable foryou.

Try to keep your back straight when you lift, use your legs to lift.

Don' t lift, twist, and turn at the same time.

Get help to lift heavy bags. Use a dolly or hand truck if necessary

OTHER SAFETY AND HEALTH PROBLEMS

Key Facts

Short - term dangers on an asbestos job can be worse than the asbestos.

Heat Stroke: a medical emergency, call an ambulance -hot skin, dry, skin, flushed skin Get the person out of the work area and into a cooler area. Take off the suit and respirator. Fan the person until help arrives. **DO NOT USE COLD WATER TO COOL THE PERSON!** If they are not unconscious, give the person a cool drink.

To prevent heat problems: Drink lots of water, Get used to the heat gradually over 2 weeks, take breaks

Chemicals: An asbestos filter on your respirator may not protect you from other chemicals.

Carbon monoxide is a dangerous gas. Signs of carbon monoxide poisoning: headache, nauseous, dizzy, sleepy, faint, nausea. Get the worker out of the work area and take off the respirator. It is very important to identify potential sources of carbon monoxide before the job begins and to eliminate them.

Electricity: An electric shock can stop your heart. If you are wet and you touch electricity, it will travel through your body. Prevent electric shocks: never use water around live wires. Shut off power and lock the electrical box. Use tools that are double insulated and grounded.

Never use metal hand tools or ladders. Use Ground Fault Circuit Interrupters (GFCI) on all circuits. If a worker has been shocked shut off the power and use a dry non-conductive pole to move the worker.

Fires: Prevent fires by: Having a worker stand by with a fire extinguisher when welding or cutting torches are used. Having an ABC rated fire extinguisher on the job.

Ladders: Inspect ladders every time you use them.

All scaffolds should have railings. Lock the wheels when people are on the scaffold. Scaffolds may not be more than 4 times higher than their minimum base dimension.

Safety and Health exercise

This is not a test. It is an exercise. Use it to see for yourself how well you understand the material in the chapter.

1. Why is electricity a hazard?

2. Why do you need Ground Fault Circuit Interrupters (GFCIs) for extension cords?

3. How do GFCIs protect against electrical shocks?

4. What other protection can you use against electrical shocks?

5. Why shouldn' t you use metal ladders?

6. Why are scaffolds on wheels dangerous?

7. How do you protect yourself from these dangers?

8. Name two common tripping hazards on asbestos jobs.

9. Why is fire safety a problem on removal jobs?

10. What type of fire extinguishers should be used on an asbestos job?

11. Why is heat stress a problem on asbestos jobs?

12. What are the symptoms of heat stress?

Discussion Questions

1. Some employers want workers to work for 6 hours without a break. Do you think this causes more heat problems than working 8 hours and taking breaks? Why do employers do it?
2. Is it necessary to drink an electrolyte drink when you are working in the heat?
3. Which do you think is safer for workers using Ground Fault Interrupters (sensitive circuit breakers) or a written Grounding Program? Why?
4. Why should a different person than the one who put it together inspect a scaffold?
5. What would you look for if you were inspecting a scaffold?

For More Information

*OSHA Electrical Standards, 29CFR1926.400 to.449

*OSHA, "Controlling Electrical Hazards," Publication No. OSHA3075.

*OSHA, "Ground Fault Protection on Construction Sites," Publication No. OSHA3007.

*OSHA Ladder Standard, 29CFR1926.450.

*OSHA Scaffold Standard, 29CFR1926.451.

*NIOSH, "General Safety Considerations," Appendix E to EPA/NIOSH, "A Guide To Respiratory Protection in the Asbestos Abatement Industry," Publication No. EPA-560-OPTS-86-001.

***Your Instructors may have a copy of these publications for you to look at.**

CHAPTER 10

MAINTENANCE - RELATED REMOVAL

Mini-Enclosures and Glove Bags

In this chapter you will learn:

About using the same methods on small and large jobs.
How to take off asbestos to repair pipes.
How to use a mini-enclosure and a glove bag.

Mini-enclosures and Glove Bags

To take off small amounts of asbestos, follow the same 6 basic rules you do on a large job.

When you take asbestos off a whole ceiling, you need to cover the whole room with 6 mil poly. You also need to do this for a whole run of pipes or air ducts, or a whole wall or floor. You need to **put up poly**, build a **decon**, and set up a **negative air machine.**

But there are lots of jobs where you only need to take off a little asbestos. It would be impractical to cover a whole room with plastic just to take asbestos cement off one pipe elbow. **But you still need to protect your self and others from the asbestos.**

You can use a **mini-enclosure** (a plastic closet) or a **glove bag** (a plastic bag with gloves built in) to do a small job. **Small jobs are usually repair jobs.**

When you do a small job you must **keep the asbestos wet, contain the work area, filter the air, use negative pressure, practice good housekeeping, set up a small decon area and properly dispose of all waste. Protect yourself with respirators that fit right and disposable suits.** On a small job, you must apply these work methods in different ways.

Mini-enclosures

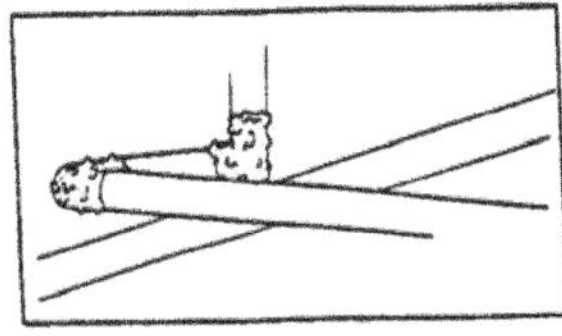

How do you take off a small patch of asbestos to hang a sprinkler pipe? You don' t have to build a full room. You can build a tiny work room - a mini-enclosure--- A Mini-enclosure is a closet like chamber you build to do asbestos work inside of. The decontamination/equipment area for a mini-enclosure is either a second enclosed chamber attached to it or can be just a piece of 6mil poly plastic on the floor just outside of the mini-enclosure. The type of decon area you use will depend on the job.

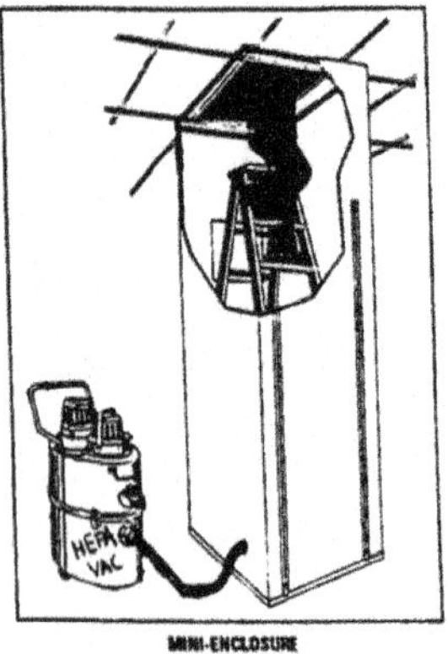

MINI-ENCLOSURE

A mini-enclosure is used for:

taking off insulation around one electrical box
taking off insulation around one outlet
taking off ceiling insulation to put up lights.
working above drop ceilings when asbestos is present
or anytime you only need to enclose a small area

When you use a mini-enclosure, follow the same six basic rules as on a large job: keep the asbestos wet, contain the work area, filter the air, use negative air pressure, practice good housekeeping, and properly dispose of waste. You must use negative air-pressure in a mini-enclosure. With a mini-enclosure, use a HEPA vacuum for negative air pressure.

A mini-enclosure looks like a plastic closet. Line a wood or plastic frame with two layers of plastic. There are also mini-enclosures that have metal frames with springs. The HEPA vacuum used for negative air pressure and filtration should be attached at the back of the mini-enclosure towards the bottom. The vacuum itself stays outside and the hose is put through the poly. The entrance from the decon area to the work area should be through a double flapped doorway just as it would be on a large job. If the decon area is enclosed, it too should have a double flapped doorway leading from the outside.

A small job is a lot like a large job. Use two layers of poly on the floor and walls of the mini-enclosure. Just like any other asbestos job, you have to wet the asbestos. You have to put it in asbestos waste bags. You have to scrub the surface clean. You have to lock down the asbestos fibers you can' t see with a lockdown sealant.

In a mini-enclosure, you need these tools:

a spray bottle for amended water
a HEPA vacuum
a labeled waste bag
scrapers
nylon bristle brushes

You may need these tools too:

- a ladder
- power tools with HEPA vacuums

A mini-enclosure does not have a full decon. **When you finish, clean off the suit with a HEPA vacuum or a damp rag. Stand on a piece of poly or in the equipment room. Wipe off your respirator. Take the suit off and put it in an asbestos waste bag.** Use one or more HEPA vacuums for negative air-pressure in a mini-enclosure. The only differences between a mini-enclosure and a large job are 1) there is not a 3 stage decon and 2) negative air pressure comes from a HEPA vacuum. When you are finished decontaminating yourself, disassemble the decon chamber or un-tape and roll up the poly on the floor and dispose of as asbestos-containing waste. **Remember: Your respirator remains on your face until the decon is disassembled and removed.**

In a mini-enclosure:

- you still have wear respirators and disposable protective suits
- you can' t eat, drink, or smoke
- you have to put up warning signs and barriers
- you have to use electricity safely

Glove Bags

A glove bag is a large plastic bag with gloves built into it. **Glove bags are good for taking off insulation around a valve, pipe elbow, or a pipe.** The asbestos inside the bag is contained. The bag is sealed air tight to the pipe. Your bare hands never touch the asbestos. You do the work through the gloves.

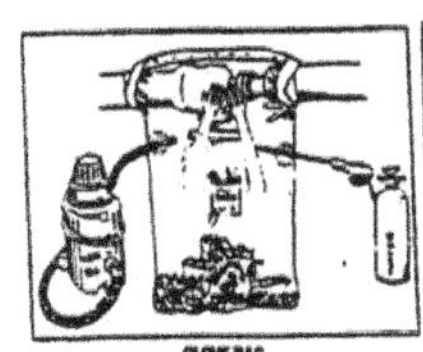
GLOVE BAG

Glove bag jobs must be done with two people!

Use a garden sprayer and a HEPA vacuum to keep asbestos out of the air. **You must wear a disposable protective suit and a PAPR or Type C pressure demand airline respirator when working with a glove bag.**

This chapter tells you how to use one glove bag to take off a small amount of asbestos. These small jobs are all maintenance jobs --you take off the asbestos so someone else can fix the pipe.

Glovebags can also be used on larger jobs but the following things must be done:

set up a negative air machine
set up a 3 stage decon
take clearance air samples
set up a full containment

Glove bags come in many sizes and shapes. They are usually made of poly with latex gloves. They have a warning label printed on them. Some companies make glove bags from thicker poly. There are special glove bags for work on vertical pipes, small pressure vessels, and for four man operations. **You may only use a glove bag once.** After you are done, dispose of it with the asbestos-containing waste. **Never move or slide the glove bag down a pipe to remove more insulation, put up a new one**.

A glove bag can only be used on a cool pipe. Poly burns at 150 degrees. Glove bags can usually be used on hot water pipes that are usually about 120 degrees or less. A glove bag cannot be used on a hot steam pipe. Steam pipes are about 300 degrees. If you take asbestos off a steam pipe, turn the steam off and let the pipe cool for at least 12 hours and then verify that the pipe is cool enough for the glove bag.

The typical glove bag is open at the top and has a tool pouch inside the bag. Some of the bags come with their sides pre cut. If not, cut the sides of the bag at the top. Attach the top of the bag to the pipe with duct tape. Next attach both the HEPA vacuum nozzle and the garden sprayer nozzle into the bag. Then put your hands inside the gloves and take off the asbestos. Asbestos doesn' t get into the air because it is trapped inside the bag.**When you are done, pull the air out of the glove bag with a HEPA vacuum. Dispose of the glove bag in a sealed asbestos waste bag.**

Just like any other asbestos job, 40% of a glove bag job is preparation

When you use a glove bag, follow the same rules you do for any job: **keep the asbestos wet, contain the work area, filter the air, and use negative air pressure.** With a glove bag, the bag contains the work and a HEPA vacuum supplies the negative air filtration. Because the HEPA vacuum will suck the air out of the bag, it should not be turned on until the job has been completed.

Just like any job, you need to clean the pipe until all the asbestos is gone. Pay attention to pipe threads and similar conditions that could retain asbestos fibers. Wash the area to clean off any asbestos. Spray a lockdown sealant. Cover up the edge of the insulation where you cut it, with a non-asbestos substitute material. Put the asbestos in a sealed, labeled waste bag.
The following illustrations go through a glove bag job step by step. Use any combination of duct tape, staples, or spray glue to seal up the bag, **as long as it is sealed totally air-tight.**

1. Put up barrier tape and warning signs.

2. Put on a PAPR respirator.

3. Put on a disposable suit.

4. Set up a decon area.

5. Deactivate HVAC system near the glove bag and lock out controls, then tape plastic over heating and ventilating system.

6. Clean the area.

7. Put a piece of poly on the floor beneath the pipe and along the wall if the pipe is near the wall.

8. Inspect the bag. Fix any holes or tears.

9. Use duct tape to strengthen the bottom of the bag. Cut a slit About 12 inches down each side of the bag (if not already pre cut).

10. Put a razor knife, nylon bristle brush, bone saw, wire cutters, lockdown sealant, paper towels, encapsulant, etc. inside the tool pouch.

11. Put tape around the pipe where you will attach the bag.

12. Tape the bag onto the tape on the pipe.

13. Fold down the top edge of the bag about one inch. Duct tape or staple it shut. Fold the stapled or taped edge down again. Tape or staple it again. Tape over the seam and all staples.

14. Fold in the sides of the bag about one inch, and staple or tape. Tape over the side seams and all the staples.

15. Tape the nozzle of the garden sprayer into the side of the bag. Tape the nozzle of the HEPA vacuum into the other side of the bag.

16. Puff ventilation smoke into the bag to check for leaks. Squeeze the bag to move the smoke around in the bag. Fix any leaks.

17. Wet the asbestos with amended water. Cut the asbestos off the pipe carefully. Continue to wet the asbestos throughout the operation. Lower the asbestos to the bottom of the glove bag.

18. Brush off all the asbestos that' s stuck to the pipe with a nylon bristled brush

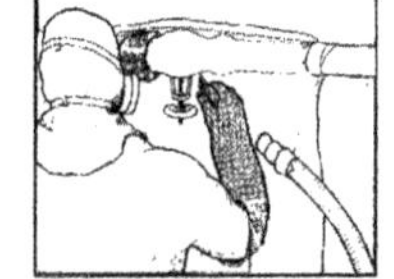

19. Rinse all the asbestos off the pipe. Rinse the sides of the bag.

20. Spray a lockdown sealant to seal the fibers you can' t see onto the pipe.

21. Seal the cut edge of the insulation with an encapsulant.

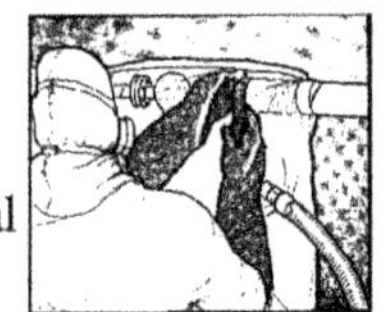

22. Grab the tools in your hands, and pull the gloves inside out. Turn on the HEPA vac and pull the air out of the bag.

23. Twist the gloves (with the tools inside) and tape them shut like an umbilical cord. Cut the gloves off the bag.

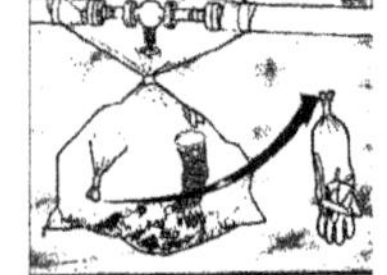

24. Turn the vacuum on again. Twist the bottom of the glove bag shut. Put tape around the twist.

25. Put a waste bag under the glove bag. With the vacuum on, carefully cut the glove bag off the pipe. Lower it into the waste bag.

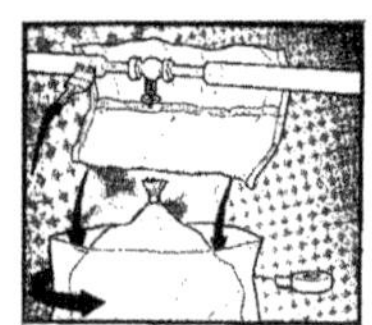

26. Cut the tape holding the vacuum hose and sprayer hose onto the bag.

27. Use the vacuum to pull the air out of the waste bag. Twist the waste bag shut. Remove the HEPA vac and tape the bag shut.

28. Fold over the top of the waste bag and tape it down (gooseneck the bag.)

29. Open up the gloves in a bucket of soapy water. Clean the tools.

30. Clean and take the poly off the floor and air vents (but not the DECON area).

31. In most cases for a small glovebag job (less than 25 linear feet), your decon area will be a piece of poly on the floor. Wet wipe and HEPA vacuum your suit and respirator. Remove your suit inside out.

32. Make sure the decon area is cleaned and disposed of as asbestos waste.

33. Seal up the poly, gloves, and suit in a waste bag.

34. Remove your respirator, making sure to cover the filters with duct tape.

35. Remove signs and barriers.

Problems with glove bags

There are some problems with glove bags. It can be clumsy to use your hands inside the gloves. When the bags get wet, it is hard to see the pipe inside. If the pipe is hot, the bags can fog up. A glove bag can melt on a hot pipe inside. The seams on the bags can leak. The gloves can tear off. Glove bags work well if the work is done right. But this is often not the case.

Whether you use a mini-enclosure or a glove bag, do all the same things you do on a large job to keep asbestos out of the air. On a small job, you just adapt those methods. Instead of a negative air machine, use a HEPA vacuum for negative air pressure. Instead of a 3 stage decon, use a piece of poly on the floor and a HEPA vacuum and damp rags to clean yourself off as long as there is no leakage or the bag doesn' t break.

Repairing asbestos

Another kind of maintenance-related work is repairing asbestos. It is usually the pipe covering or jacket that is repaired, not the friable asbestos itself. (Sprayed-on insulation can't be repaired.) **You must wear a respirator when doing repairs. You will also need to wear a protective suit. Repairs are usually done by putting a canvas or fiberglass patch over the torn jacket or covering. Sometimes it is necessary to patch a hole in the insulation itself.** Mastic, encapsulant, or glue is painted over the patch. You may use fiberglass that has glue already in it (wettable cloth). Dipping the patch in water activates the glue. All repairs should be done inside a glove bag or mini-enclosure. For large repairs (more than 25 feet long or 10 feet square), use a negative pressure machine, put poly on the walls and floor, and build a 3 stage decon. A large-scale repair is just like any other large job. If you have to remove crumbling plaster or other materials to do a small repair, use a mini-enclosure. Use a HEPA vacuum to clean any dust off the surface. Mist the torn covering with amended water. Be careful not to tear the asbestos or the covering. Work carefully and make the patch airtight.

MAINTENANCE-RELATED REMOVAL
Mini-enclosures and Glove Bags

Key Facts

To take off small amounts of asbestos, follow the same 6 rules you do on a large job:

keep the asbestos wet
contain the work
filter the air with HEPA filters
use a HEPA vacuum for negative air pressure
practice good housekeeping
properly cleanup and dispose of all waste

When you work on a small job, you must wear a PAPR respirator and a disposable suit

A mini-enclosure is the same as a full containment without a 3-stage decontamination unit.

Use a HEPA vacuum for negative air pressure in a mini-enclosure.

A glove bag will melt on a pipe above 120 degrees F.

With a glove bag, your hands never touch the asbestos inside the bag.

When you are done, pull the air out of the glove bag with a HEPA vacuum.

Throw out the glove bag in a sealed, labeled asbestos waste bag.

Glove bag exercise

This is not a test. It is an exercise on the use of the glove bag. Use it to see for yourself how well you understand the procedures for safely doing glove bag removal of asbestos insulation. Read over all of the steps below. Put these steps on order by writing a number in the space before each item to show the order in which each step would be performed.

_____ Pre-Clean the area

_____ Put tape around the pipe where you will attach the bag. Staple and tape the glove bag closed.

_____ Reinforce the bottom of the bag with tape. Cut about a foot down the sides of the glove bag (if not already pre cut). Place tools inside the pouch.

_____ Put on a respirator and disposable suit. Do a negative and positive pressure fit check.

_____ Put up barriers and hang asbestos warning signs.

_____ Cut two small holes in the bag and insert the nozzles of the HEPA vacuum and the sprayer. Seal the openings with duct tape. Smoke test the bag to ensure that it is sealed airtight.

_____ Set up a DECON area.

_____ Break the insulation away from the pipe and lower it to the bottom of the bag.

_____ Put poly under the pipe and also up the wall if the pipe is close to the wall.

_____ Spray the inside of the bag with water to wash any asbestos to the bottom of the bag.

_____ Deactivate HVAC system and lock out controls, then tape plastic over vent.

_____ Spray the insulation with amended water, being sure to soak the area to be cut.

_____ Cut the insulation with a bone or camper saw at each end of the section to be removed.

_____ Put encapsulant paint on the cut edges of the asbestos on the pipe.

_____ Clean and remove poly under pipe and on wall.

_____ Grab the tools in your hands and pull the gloves inside out. Remove the rest of the air in the bag by briefly turning on the HEPA vacuum. Twist the sleeve and tie it off with two pieces of duct tape. Cut the sleeve at the twist. Put the sleeve containing the tools in the next glove bag to be used or open it in a pail of water for cleaning.

_____ Spray, scrub, and wipe the exposed pipe to remove any asbestos on the pipe. Use a brush with nylon or fiber bristles. Spray lockdown on the pipe.

_____ Vacuum the work area and your clothes.

_____ Remove rope and signs from the work area.

_____ Turn the HEPA vacuum on again. Twist the bag below the pipe and tape it closed.

_____ Slip a large plastic disposal bag around the glove bag. Remove the glove bag from the pipe and fold it into the disposal bag. Seal and label the bag.

_____ Wipe your respirator with a damp cloth. Remove your suit inside out and place it in a disposal bag with contaminated rags and used filters. Seal and label the bag for disposal. Remove your respirator.

_____ Clean and remove DECON area.

Discussion Questions

1. When you use a HEPA vacuum for negative air pressure in a mini-enclosure, where do you put it? At the top of the mini-enclosure? At the bottom? In the decon room?
2. How do you use a mini-enclosure to string cables above a drop ceiling? Do you need an enclosure at both ends? How can you set up negative air pressure?
3. What kind of enclosure would you use to take asbestos off one small boiler in a large basement?
4. How would you set up negative air pressure on this job? How would you decontaminate?

For more information

* OSHA Asbestos Standard, 29 CFR 1926.1101

*** Your instructor may have a copy for you to look at.**

GLOSSARY

ABATEMENT:	Lessening the HAZARD of ASBESTOS. Includes ENCAPSULATION, ENCLOSURE, REPAIR, and REMOVAL of ASBESTOS.
ACOUSTICAL INSULATION:	The general application or use of asbestos for the control of sound due to its lack of reverberant surfaces.
AEROSOL:	Particles, either solid or liquid, suspended in air.
AGGRESSIVE SAMPLING:	A way of taking AIR SAMPLES where the air is stirred up using fans and leaf blowers. Aggressive sampling is used for CLEARANCE AIR SAMPLES.
AHERA:	The Asbestos Hazard Emergency Response Act - The EPA law covering ASBESTOS in schools.
AIHA:	American Industrial Hygiene Association.
AIHA ACCREDITED LABORATORY:	A certification given by AIHA to an analytical laboratory that has successfully participated in the Proficiency Analytical Testing (PAT) program for quality control as established by the National Institute for Occupational Safety & Health.
AIR CELL:	Insulation normally used on pipes and ductwork comprised of corrugated cardboard and frequently impregnated with asbestos fibers.
AIR LOCK:	An empty room/space located between the CHANGE ROOM and the SHOWER ROOM and the SHOWER ROOM and the EQUIPMENT ROOM in some DECONS. Workers pass through the double flapped doors one at a time.
AIR MONITORING:	The process of measuring the fiber content within a specific volume of air.
AIR PLENUM:	Any space used to convey air in a building or structure. The space above a suspended ceiling is often used as an air plenum.

AIR-PURIFYING RESPIRATOR: A piece of protective equipment, which is a facemask with filters that you wear. It filters or purifies the air before the worker inhales it.

AIR SAMPLING: Measuring the amount of ASBESTOS in the air using a pump.

AIR-SUPPLIED RESPIRATOR: A protective face mask that supplies clean air to you from outside the work area via a hose, using a compressor, or air tanks.

ALVEOLI: Tiny air sacs found in your lungs. They are important areas where the gas exchange occurs.

AMBIENT AIR: The surrounding air or atmosphere in a given area under normal conditions.

AMENDED WATER: Water plus a chemical called a SURFACTANT. Amended water soaks into ASBESTOS faster than plain water.

AMOSITE: An asbestiform mineral of the amphibole group containing approximately 50% silicon and 40% iron III oxide, made of straight, brittle, fibers that are pale gray to pale brown in color.

ANSI: American National Standards Institute

APPROVED LANDFILL: A site for disposing of asbestos containing waste that is licensed and follows EPA guidelines.

AREA AIR SAMPLE: An AIR SAMPLE taken from one spot in a room. It is used for measuring how much ASBESTOS is in the area during work.

ASBESTOS: A naturally occurring mineral used for insulation in many buildings. Asbestos breaks into FIBERS. It causes lung cancer and other diseases. Varieties regulated by OSHA and EPA are chrysotile, crocidolite, amosite, anthophylite, actinolite, and tremolite.

ASBESTOS ABATEMENT: Procedures to reduce fiber release from asbestos-containing materials in buildings.

ASBESTOS FIBERS: Fibers generated from asbestos-containing materials with their length being greater than 5 microns and a length to width ratio of at least 3:1.

ASBESTOS STANDARD: Reference to the OSHA requirements in the general industry and construction standards regarding asbestos exposure (29 CFR 1910.1001, 29CFR 1926.1101) and EPA requirements (NESHAP, AHERA, and ASHARA).

ASBESTOS-CONTAINING MATERIAL (ACM): Any material containing more than 1% by weight of asbestos of any type or mixture of types.

ASBESTOS-CONTAINING WASTE MATERIAL: Any material, which is or is suspected of being asbestos or any material contaminated asbestos, which is to be removed from a work area for disposal.

ASBESTOSIS: A disease caused by ASBESTOS. It is the scarring of the lungs, also known as white lung.

AUTHORIZED PERSON: Any person authorized by the employer and required by work duties to be present in regulated areas.

B READER: A doctor who has had special training and has been certified to identify signs of occupational diseases on X-rays.

BARRIER: Any surface that seals off the work area to inhibit the movement of fibers.

BREATHING ZONE: A hemisphere forward of the shoulders with a radius of approximately 6 to 9 inches.

BRONCHI: Two main branches of the windpipe where air travels to your lungs.

BUILDING/FACILITY OWNER: The legal entity, including a lessee, which exercises control over management and record keeping functions relating to a building and/or facility.

BULK SAMPLE: A thumbnail sized piece of material, which is sent to a lab to test it for ASBESTOS.

CANCER: A large group of diseases where cells grow abnormally, rapidly and out of control.

CARBON MONOXIDE: A colorless, odorless, tasteless poisonous gas.

CARTRIDGE: A filter used on an AIR-PURIFYING RESPIRATOR.

CERTIFIED INDUSTRIAL HYGIENIST (C.I.H.): An industrial hygienist, who after successfully passing an examination in the comprehensive practice of industrial hygiene, is certified by the American Board of Industrial Hygiene (ABIH).

CILIA: Very tiny hairs that line the walls of your windpipe and BRONCHI. They beat automatically and move mucus up your windpipe to remove objects from your respiratory system.

CLASS I ASBESTOS WORK: Activities involving the removal of Thermal System Insulation (TSI) and Surfacing ACM or PACM as defined by OSHA.

CLASS II ASBESTOS WORK: Activities involving the removal of ACM that is not TSI or surfacing material as defined by OSHA. This includes, but is not limited to, the removal of asbestos-containing wallboard, floor tile and sheeting, roofing and siding shingles, and construction mastics.

CLASS III ASBESTOS WORK: Repair and maintenance operations, where "ACM," including thermal system insulation and surfacing material, is likely to be disturbed as defined by OSHA.

CLASS IV ASBESTOS WORK: Housekeeping (not clean up) that takes place after a Class I, II, or III job has been completed. Does not include picking up and bagging of asbestos debris/dust during Class I, II, or III operations as defined by OSHA.

CLEAN ROOM: The last room in the DECON (going out) which is uncontaminated. Has facilities for the storage of employees' street clothing and uncontaminated materials and equipment.

CLEARANCE AIR SAMPLE: An AREA AIR SAMPLE taken at the end of an abatement job. It tells the building owner whether the room has been cleaned adequately after the asbestos removal.

CLOSELY RESEMBLE: Means that the major workplace conditions, which have contributed to the levels of historic asbestos exposure, are no more protective than conditions of the current workplace.

COMPETENT PERSON: In the OSHA regulations, a trained supervisor who makes sure that rules are followed and equipment works, is capable of identifying existing asbestos hazards in the workplace and selecting the appropriate control strategy for asbestos exposure; and who has the authority to take prompt corrective measures to eliminate them.

In addition, for Class I and Class II work, is specially trained in a training course which meets the criteria for EPA' s Model Accreditation Plan (40 CR 763) for **project designer** or **supervisor**, or its equivalent; and for Class III and Class IV work, is trained in an operations and Maintenance (O&M) course developed by EPA [40 CFR 763.92 (a)(2)].

CONTAINMENT: Isolating the work area from the rest of the building. Usually done by putting POLY on the walls and floors and using a NEGATIVE AIR MACHINE. This keeps ASBESTOS FIBERS inside the work area.

CONTRACT MANAGER or DESIGNEE: The person assigned to be responsible for certain defined functions in administering the Contract, and is the only authorized person to make certain decisions, such as, but not limited to: approving deviations from technical Contract requirements and approving changes to the Contract sum.

CONTROL METHODS: Ways of controlling ASBESTOS. Includes ENCAPSULATION, ENCLOSURE, REPAIR, REMOVAL, RESTRICTION, and O&M.

CRITICAL BARRIER: Airtight barrier, usually 2 layers of 6 mil sheet plastic, which separates the contaminated work area from any other air space. Installed first, this barrier covers items such as, but not limited to: windows, doors, HVAC components, floor drains, and containment walls.

CHRYSOTILE: The only asbestiform mineral of the serpentine group, which contains approximately 40% each of silica and magnesium oxide. It is the most commonly used form of asbestos in buildings.

CUBIC CENTIMETER: A space about the size of a sugar cube. Asbestos in the air is measured in FIBERs per Cubic Centimeter.

DECONTAMINATION UNIT or AREA (DECON): The DECON has three enclosed rooms consisting of the DIRTY (EQUIPMENT) ROOM, SHOWER ROOM, and CLEAN ROOM that are adjacent to and connected to the regulated area. Everyone must enter and leave the work/regulated area through the DECON.

DEMOLITION: The wrecking or taking out/removal, together with any related handling operations, of any building component, system, finish, or assembly and any related razing or stripping of asbestos products within the building.

DIRTY ROOM: The last room in the DECON (going in). Workers take their suits off in the dirty room on their way to the shower. Dirty hard hats and tools are also stored there. Also called: EQUIPMENT ROOM.

DISPOSAL BAG: A properly labeled, 6 mil thick, leak-tight plastic bag used for transporting asbestos waste from the abatement work area to a disposal site.

DISTURBANCE: Contact, which releases fibers from ACM or PACM or debris, containing ACM or PACM. This term includes activities that disrupt the matrix of ACM or PACM, render ACM or PACM friable, or generate visible debris as defined by OSHA. DISTURBANCE includes cutting away small amounts of ACM or PACM, no greater than the amount that can be contained in one standard sized glove bag or waste bag in order to access a building component. In no event shall the amount of ACM or PACM so disturbed exceed that which can be contained in one glove bag or waste bag which shall not exceed 60 inches in length and width.

DOSE: The amount of a substance that you are exposed to during a specific time period.

DOSE-RELATED: A relationship between the amount of a substance you are exposed to and the reaction your body has to that exposure.

DUCT TAPE: Sticky, often silver colored tape. Used to attach POLY among other uses.

DUST MASK: Also known as a filtering facepiece usually made of paper or other fibrous material. It is not legal for ASBESTOS work. It does not provide adequate respiratory protection against asbestos fibers because they don't fit tightly to the face.

ELECTRON MICROSCOPE: A microscope, which beams electrons (instead of light) at a sample. Electron microscopes are more exact than LIGHT MICROSCOPEs.

EMPLOYEE NOTIFICATION: Informing employees and building occupants of the presence of asbestos within their building. They also must be informed of the hazards associated with asbestos exposure, what is being done to eliminate the hazards, etc.

ENCAPSULANT: A material that surrounds or embeds asbestos fibers in an adhesive matrix and prevents release of fibers.

Removal encapsulant: a penetrating encapsulant specifically designed for removal of asbestos-containing materials rather that for encapsulation in place.

Bridging encapsulant: an encapsulant that forms a discrete layer on the surface of an asbestos matrix.

Penetrating encapsulant: an encapsulant that is absorbed by the asbestos matrix without leaving a discrete surface layer.

Lockdown encapsulant: an encapsulant that is used after asbestos has been removed from the substrate to "lockdown" any stray asbestos fibers.

ENCAPSULATION: Treatment of asbestos-containing materials, with an encapsulant.

ENCLOSE: To build an airtight barrier around ASBESTOS. A way to control ASBESTOS without removing it.

ENCLOSURE: The construction of an airtight, impermeable, permanent barrier around asbestos-containing material to control the release of asbestos fibers into the air.

ENGINEERING CONTROLS: Ways of controlling airborne levels of asbestos such as, building barriers, using negative air ventilation systems, etc. Are to be determined and utilized before RESPIRATORs may be used.

ENVIRONMENTAL PROTECTION AGENCY / EPA: A U.S. government agency that protects the environment and citizens from pollution.

EQUIPMENT ROOM / CHANGE ROOM: A contaminated room located within the decontamination area (the chamber closest to the work area) that is supplied with impermeable bags or containers for the disposal of contaminated protective clothing and equipment.

EXPOSURE: The amount of ASBESTOS fibers in the air within a worker' s breathing zone determined by air monitoring and calculated as if the worker was not wearing a respirator.

FIBER: A single strand of ASBESTOS. ASBESTOS fibers are so small they are invisible to the naked eye. From the OSHA standard, it must be at least 5 microns long with a length-to-width aspect ratio of 3 to 1.

FIBER CONTROL: Minimizing the amount of asbestos fiber generation through the application of amended water onto asbestos-containing materials, or enclosure (isolation) of the material.

FIBERS PER CUBIC CENTIMETER (F/CC): The unit of measure of reporting the concentration of airborne ASBESTOS fibers in the air. A pump pulls contaminated air through a filter. The number of FIBERs on the filter are counted by using a microscope. The amount of air is measured in CUBIC CENTIMETERS.

FIBROSIS: A disease where scar tissue is formed in the connective tissue of the lungs.

FILTER: A media component used in respirators, HEPA vacuums, negative air machines, and air samples to remove solid or liquid particles from the air.

FITTING: Any valve, tee, elbow, flange, union, reducer, or other piping connector within any piping system, which may be insulated with asbestos.

FRIABLE ASBESTOS MATERIAL: Material that contains more than 1% asbestos by weight, and that can be crumbled, pulverized, or reduced to powder by hand pressure when dry.

FULL-FACE RESPIRATOR: A facemask that covers the full area of your face from the hairline of your forehead to under your chin.

GLOVEBAG: A sack (typically constructed of 6 mil transparent polyethylene or polyvinyl chloride plastic) with two inward projecting long sleeve gloves, which are designed to enclose an object from which an asbestos-containing material is removed.

GRADE D AIR: Air for an AIR-SUPPLIED RESPIRATOR. Grade D air has specific maximum levels of specific chemical gases, oil, and water filtered out so that it is safe to breathe.

GROUND FAULT CIRCUIT INTERRUPTER (GFCI): A sensitive circuit breaker for tools, equipment, and extension cords. A GFCI will stop the flow of electrical current before the worker is shocked or electrocuted. Must be used for all asbestos abatement jobs because water is present.

HALF-MASK RESPIRATOR: A facemask that covers half of your face. It covers your nose and mouth from the bridge of your nose to your chin.

HAZARD: A danger or a risk from an unsafe or unhealthy condition.

HEAT STRESS: An illness caused by working in a hot area. Has 3 levels or degrees of effect, which are HEAT CRAMPS, HEAT EXHAUSTION, and HEAT STROKE. HEAT STROKE is the most serious and may necessitate a medical emergency because of a body's inability to cool itself.

HEPA FILTER VACUUM COLLECTION EQUIPMENT (or vacuum cleaner): High efficiency particulate air filtered vacuum collection equipment with a filter system capable of collecting and retaining asbestos fibers. Filters should be 99.97% efficient at retaining fibers of 0.3 microns or larger.

HIGH-EFFICIENCY PARTICULATE AIR FILTER (HEPA): A filter which removes from air 99.97% or more of monodispersed dioctyl phthalate (DOP) particles having a mean particle diameter of 0.3 micrometer.

HVAC SYSTEM: **H**eating, **V**entilation, and **A**ir **C**onditioning system.

IMMEDIATELY DANGEROUS to LIFE or HEALTH: A condition where a hazardous atmosphere exists and exposure to the condition will result in serious injury or death in a very short time.

LATENCY PERIOD: The time from first exposure to disease development; e.g. cancer.

LOCAL EXHAUST VENTILATION: The mechanical removal of air contaminants from the point of operation.

LUNG CANCER: An uncontrolled growth of cells in the lungs, which could result in the death of the host.

LOCK-OUT/TAG-OUT (LOTO): Installation of a locking or tagging device to prevent activation of an electrical circuit or mechanical system, which has been deactivated for safety reasons. Always utilized in conjunction with established procedures by those employees who have access to these energized systems. Refer to OSHA 29 CFR 1910.147, "Control of Hazardous Energy Source."

MEDICAL HISTORY: A record of a person's past health, including all the hazardous materials that they might have been exposed to and also any injuries or illnesses which might dictate their future health status.

MDE: Maryland Department of the Environment

MESOTHELIOMA: A relatively rare form of cancer, which develops in the chest or abdominal lining with no known cure.

METHOD 7400: NIOSH sampling and analytical method for fibers using phase contrast microscopy.

MICRON: One millionth of a meter.

MIL: Prefix meaning one thousand. One thousandth of a meter.

MINERAL WOOL: A commonly used substitute for asbestos.

MOSH: Maryland Occupational Safety & Health

MSDS: Material Safety Data Sheet

MUCO-CILIARY ESCALATOR: One of the body's defense mechanisms against asbestos. Consists of tiny hair cells called cilia and mucus, which are in the windpipe. Upon breathing, fibers attach to the mucus and an upward movement of the cilia transfer the fibers and mucus to the throat where the mixture is either coughed out or swallowed.

NEGATIVE EXPOSURE ASSESSMENT: Demonstration by objective data, or by prior and representative sampling data, or by initial exposure monitoring that employee exposures during an operation are expected to be consistently below the PELs.

NESHAP: National Emission Standard for Hazardous Air Pollutants, EPA Regulation 40 CFR Part 61 subpart M,

NIOSH: National Institute for Occupational Safety & Health
The official approving agency for respiratory protective equipment that tests and certifies respirators.

NEGATIVE PRESSURE: An atmosphere created in the work area enclosure such that airborne fibers will tend to be drawn through the filtration system rather than leak out into the surrounding areas. The air pressure inside the work area is less than outside the work area.

NEGATIVE PRESSURE USER SEAL CHECK: One of two fit checks to test the seal of a respirator to a wearer' s face. The checkinvolves covering and sealing the filter openings/inhalation valves, and sucking in. The respirator should collapse slightly against the face.

NEGATIVE PRESSURE RESPIRATOR: A respirator in which the air pressure inside the respirator inlet covering is positive during exhalation in relation to the air pressure on the outside; and negative during inhalation in relation to the air pressure on the outside of the respirator.

NEGATIVE PRESSURE VENTILATION SYSTEM: A pressure differential ventilation system consisting of a housing holding a fan and motor; a series of filters which clean contaminated air. It ventilates this air to another location, which creates a negative pressure differential.

OIL LESS COMPRESSOR: An air compressor that is not oil lubricated and does not allow carbon monoxide to be generated in the breathing air.

O&M PLAN / OPERATIONS AND MAINTENANCE PLAN: A plan for controlling the ASBESTOS that remains in a building. This plan includes:

1) Where asbestos is found in the building. ACM may need to be labeled.
2) The amount of training that workers must receive to work with the material.
3) A permit which must be obtained before working with asbestos.
4) Accepted ways to work with asbestos safely. This includes equipment, worker protection, training, and medical exams.
5) When and how to check the condition of asbestos materials and record any changes.

OSHA / OCCUPATIONAL SAFETY AND HEALTH ADMINISTRATION: The Occupational Safety & Health Administration. A U.S. government agency within the Department of Labor that regulates worker safety and health on the job.

OSHA STANDARD: An OSHA regulation, for example, the OSHA Asbestos Standard, 29 CFR 1926.1101.

PARTICULATE CONTAMINANTS: Minute airborne particles given off in the form of dusts, smoke, fumes, or mists.

PACM / PRESUMED ASBESTOS-CONTAINING MATERIAL: Thermal system insulation and surfacing material found in buildings constructed no later than 1980.

PAPR / POWERED AIR PURIFYING RESPIRATOR: An air-purifying respirator (a facemask with a filter) that has a motor. Contaminated air is pulled through filters where it is cleaned; the clean air goes to the face piece. Level II employees are required to wear this type of respirator or an AIRLINE/SUPPLIED AIR RESPIRATOR while working with asbestos.

PCM / PHASE CONTRAST MICROSCOPY: The analytical laboratory method used to count asbestos fibers for area and personal air samples.

PELs / PERMISSIBLE EXPOSURE LIMITS: **(for asbestos)** The OSHA PELs are 0.1 fibers per cubic centimeter of air as an 8-hour Time-Weighted Average (TWA) and 1.0 fiber per cubic centimeter of air within any 30-minute period of an 8-hour day called the Excursion Limit (EL).

PERSONAL AIR SAMPLE: An AIR SAMPLE taken in a worker' s breathingzone. This is a measure of how much asbestos the worker is exposed to. Personal air samples must be taken on a percentage of workers during every day according to the OSHA Standard on Asbestos, 29 CFR 1926.1101.

PERSONAL MONITORING: Sampling of the asbestos fiber concentrations within the breathing zone of an employee.

PERSONAL PROTECTIVE EQUIPMENT: Any material or device worn to protect a worker from exposure to, or contact with any harmful material or force.

PLM / POLARIZED LIGHT MICROSCOPY: The analytical laboratory method used on BULK SAMPLES of asbestos, which is reported as a percentage of asbestos to the total sample.

PIPE LAGGING: The insulation wrapping around a pipe.

POLY or POLYETHYLENE SHEET PLASTIC: Six-mil sheet plastic taped to walls and floors to prevent ASBESTOS from contaminating other outside areas.

POSITIVE-PRESSURE USER SEAL CHECK: One of two fit checks to test the seal of your RESPIRATOR to your face. You check for leaks by covering the exhalation valve(s) with your hands and blowing into the face piece without breaking the seal; the mask puffs out. Once the mask puffs out, hold your breath and sense for leaks.

POSTING: Refers to danger or notification signs, which must be posted in any area in which asbestos removal is occurring, or at the entrance to the building where such work is taking place.

PRESSURE-DEMAND AIR-SUPPLIED RESPIRATOR: A facemask with air supplied to the mask through a hose from outside the work area via compressor, bottled air, or an air pump. The amount of air that is supplied to you is based on what you need to breathe. A regulator senses the amount of air that you need to breathe.

PRIMARY BARRIER: Sheet plastic barriers installed after critical barriers, which protect building components and non-movable objects from water damage and asbestos contamination. The primary barrier is normally two independent and overlapped sheets.

PROTECTION FACTOR: The ratio of the ambient concentration of an airborne substance to the concentration of the substance inside a sealed respirator. The protection factor is a measure of the degree of protection provided by a respirator to the wearer.

PROTECTIVE CLOTHING: Protective lightweight disposable garments such as Tyvek or Kleenguard worn by workers performing asbestos abatement to keep gross contamination off their body.

PULMONARY FUNCTION TEST: A breathing test to see how well your lungs are working. It measures how much air you can breathe in and out. It can tell you if there is a problem with your lungs.

PURPLE BOOK: EPA publication June 1985 entitled Guidance for Controlling Asbestos-Containing Materials in Buildings, 1985 edition.

QUALITATIVE FIT TEST: A test that tells you if you have any leaks in your RESPIRATOR. You are tested by someone who follows the OSHA protocol. The test uses an irritant smoke, banana oil, or saccharin. If you smell or taste the testing substance, you have a leak which means the respirator does not fit. You must have a qualitative fit test for any NEGATIVE-PRESSURE RESPIRATOR that is issued to you.

QUANTITATIVE FIT TEST: A test that tells you if you have any leaks in your RESPIRATOR. It is a more accurate test. A probe and analytical equipment is used to determine the amount of testing agent inside the mask and compares this inside level to the amount of testing agent outside of the mask. It gives you a personal PROTECTION FACTOR for the respirator you use.

RECORD KEEPING: Detailed documentation of all program activities, decisions, analyses, and any other pertinent information regarding asbestos management.

REGULATED AREA: According to OSHA, an area established by the employer to demarcate areas where Class I, Class II, and Class III asbestos work is being conducted, and any adjoining area where debris and waste from such asbestos work may accumulate; and a work area within which airborne concentrations of asbestos, exceed or there is a reasonable possibility they may exceed, the permissible exposure limits.

REMOVAL: All operations where ACM and/or PACM are taken out or stripped from structures or substrates, and includes demolition operations.

REPAIR: Returning damaged ACM to an undamaged condition to prevent fiber release.

RESPIRATOR: A device designed to protect the wearer from the inhalation of harmful contaminants. Must be approved by NIOSH and used in accordance with the employer's respiratory protection program and manufacturer's procedures.

RESPIRATOR PROGRAM: A written program established by an employer who provides for the safe use of respirators on their job sites.

RESTRICTION: An area of a building or an entire building that has RESTRICTED ACCESS to only those Level II employees who wear a RESPIRATOR and DISPOSABLE PROTECTIVE CLOTHING.

SCBA / SELF-CONTAINED, BREATHING APPARATUS: An AIR-SUPPLIED RESPIRATOR in which you carry the air supply in a high-pressure tank.

SECONDARY BARRIER: 6 mil sheet plastic installed on floors and walls of a containment during removal activities to protect primary layers.

SHOWER ROOM: A room between the equipment and clean rooms in a worker decontamination system in which workers shower when leaving the work area.

SPRAYBACK: New insulation put up ceiling surfaces, columns, and beams after ASBESTOS is removed and the job passes the CLEARANCE AIR SAMPLE.

STRUCTURAL MEMBER: Any load supporting member such as beams and load supporting walls of a building.

SUBSTRATE: The material or existing surface located under or behind the asbestos-containing material.

SURFACING MATERIAL: Material that is sprayed, troweled-on or otherwise applied to surfaces (such as acoustical plaster on ceilings and fireproofing materials on structural members, or other materials on surfaces for acoustical, fireproofing, and other purposes).

SURFACTANT: A chemical wetting agent added to water to improve penetration into an asbestos-containing material, thus reducing the quantity of water required for a given operation or area. Breaks down the surface tension of water.

SURGICAL REMOVAL: A process by which small amounts of asbestos are removed with extreme care from substrates to which critical barriers or other seals are to be applied. This process usually involves scraping with small hand tools directly into the inlet of a HEPA vacuum

TEM / TRANSMISSION ELECTRON MICROSCOPY: The analytical laboratory method to identify asbestos fibers in an air sample. It is the most accurate test because it only identifies asbestos fibers and is reported by the lab as "structures per square millimeter" or "s/mm^2" of air that is sampled.

TESTING LABORATORY: An entity engaged to perform specific inspections or tests of the work, either at the project site or elsewhere; and to report and (if required) interpret results of those inspections or tests.

TIME-WEIGHTED AVERAGE (TWA): The average concentration of a contaminant in air during a specific time period.

THERMAL SYSTEM INSULATION (TSI): ACM applied to pipes, fittings, boilers, breaching, tanks, ducts or other structural components to prevent heat loss or gain.

TYPE C RESPIRATOR: An AIR-SUPPLIED RESPIRATOR.

WATER DAMAGE: Deterioration or delamination of wall, ceiling, flooring or other materials due to leaks from plumbing or cracks in the roof or floor.

WET CLEANING: The process of eliminating asbestos contamination from building surfaces and objects by using cloths, mops, or other cleaning utensils which have been dampened with amended water or diluted removal encapsulant and afterwards thoroughly decontaminated or disposed of as asbestos-contaminated waste.

WHITE BLOOD CELLS: Also known as Phagocytes. A part of the body's defense system. They attack foreign objects like bacteria or ASBESTOS.

WORK AREA: The area where asbestos-related work or removal operations are performed which is designed and/or isolated to prevent the spread of asbestos dust, fibers or debris, and entry by unauthorized personnel. Work area is a Regulated Area as defined by 29 CFR 1926.1101.

WORK HISTORY: Part of a medical exam. Lists what you have worked with, when, and where. This helps the doctor look for job-related diseases that you might have.

WORK PRACTICES: Ways of doing work that affect how safe it is. For example, keeping ASBESTOS wet is a good work practice. It keeps ASBESTOS out of the air.

VISIBLE EMISSIONS: Any emissions containing particulate asbestos material that are visually detectable without the aid of instruments.

VISUAL INSPECTION: A walk-through type of inspection by the competent person and/or the building owner's representative to detect incomplete work, damage, or inadequate cleanup.